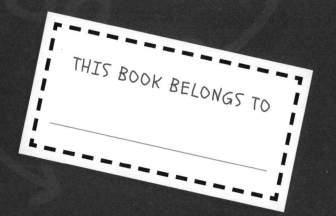

THIS BOOK BELONGS TO

_____

The Middle School Rules of

VONTAE DAVIS

as told by *Sean Jensen*

BroadStreet
PUBLISHING

BroadStreet Kids
Savage, Minnesota, USA.
BroadStreet Kids is an imprint of BroadStreet Publishing® Group, LLC.
www.broadstreetpublishing.com

The Middle School Rules of Vontae Davis

© 2019 Vontae Davis and Sean Jensen

Illustrated by Daniel Smith.
Back cover photo courtesy of Polina Osherov I polinaosherov.com

978-1-4245-5587-1 (hard cover)
978-1-4245-5588-8 (e-book)

Cover and interior design by Garborg Design Works I garborgdesign.com
Editorial services provided by Ginger Garrett I gingergarrett.com
and Michelle Winger I literallyprecise.com

Printed in China.

19 20 21 22 23   5 4 3 2 1

ACKNOWLEDGMENTS

from Vontae Davis

I want to thank Grandma Adaline for being in my life, and for having such a positive influence on the seven kids you raised.

Thanks to my wife, Megan, for being so supportive.
I'm excited about our future together, raising a family,
and reading this book to our children.

Thank you, Brian Bradtke, for introducing me to Sean Jensen
and making this possible.

Thanks to everyone who did interviews for this book to really bring my childhood to life, including Coach Craig.

I am grateful for the help of my siblings, especially Vernon who wrote the foreword and encouraged me to tell my story.

from Sean Jensen

I thank God for His love, and His mercy and grace.

I thank my wife Erica for her love and support,
and my children Elijah and Zarah for inspiring me.

Thank you Brian Bradtke of B2 Enterprises for initially introducing me to Vontae. And thank you Vontae for your transparency and passion to tell your story to inspire children. Our first time together—over sushi in Chicago—was special, as was our trip to D.C.
to visit with your family, including Grandma!

I also want to thank Daniel Smith for his amazing artwork;
it has been a privilege to get to know you and work with you.
Lastly, I want to thank our team at BroadStreet Publishing
for having my back!

Dear Reader,

I had a tough childhood. You're going to read that in my Middle School Rules book.

But I want you to read this book and see hope throughout my story. No matter what circumstances you find yourself in, you will have the strength and faith to use some of the lessons I learned to keep pushing forward. I was inspired to be as vulnerable as possible because many of you could be facing similar situations.

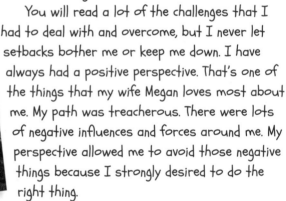

You will read a lot of the challenges that I had to deal with and overcome, but I never let setbacks bother me or keep me down. I have always had a positive perspective. That's one of the things that my wife Megan loves most about me. My path was treacherous. There were lots of negative influences and forces around me. My perspective allowed me to avoid those negative things because I strongly desired to do the right thing.

I knew so many kids who had as much talent as I had, but they couldn't resist the bad influences. It was hard for me too, but I had many strong people around me, and they allowed me to flourish. Sometimes it's difficult to do the right thing. People might make fun of you or choose not to be your friend anymore. But deep down inside, you know what's right, and you have to possess the strength to do that no matter what the cost.

I am so grateful to my grandmother for many things—one of them is what she did every night. She went into her "war room," which was actually just her bedroom, and she prayed for people, including her children and grandchildren. I know those prayers made a difference in my life.

Before I headed off to the University of Illinois, my Grandmother told me to memorize and recite Psalm 23 before stepping onto the football field. That impacted the way I played the game.

I hope you enjoy my story,

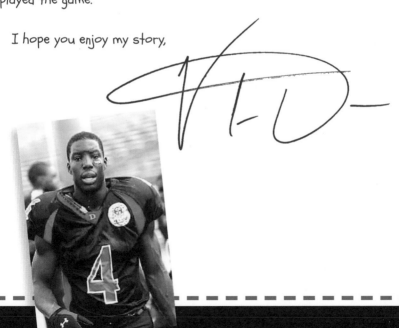

FOREWORD

I knew Vontae was special when he was young. He would play a football video game all the time, so he knew a lot about the sport. I don't want to say it made me jealous, but it did make me really look at him like a football guru! He knew about every player, and I didn't know anything about football because I played so much basketball.

We didn't grow up in a great neighborhood. There was a lot of crime and it wasn't the best situation for leadership or influence. But our grandmother raised us, and a lot of the qualities she instilled in me, Vontae has too. I recognized that early on. I knew I had to be a role model for my younger siblings. I mean, being the oldest, I knew they all looked up to me.

We learned, "The right thing to do, is to do the right thing." But it was still extremely hard to do the right thing because of our environment. Sometimes, I would get in trouble and do the wrong thing. Then, I would get my mind right because I wanted to be successful in life.

I remember when Vontae was drafted. I was so proud of him for staying on the right path and doing things the right way. It was even better that he was selected in the first round! It's humbling that I have a younger brother who followed in my footsteps.

I hope readers pay attention to Vontae's story. They can learn that Vontae was a regular kid with goals and ambitions. It's motivational and inspiring when you think about how the six of us were raised by our grandmother. Vontae's life is proof that no matter what you go through or where you come from, if you set goals and listen—and he listened to our grandmother! —you can become successful.

Vernon Davis (Vontae's big brother)

TABLE OF CONTENTS

Chapter 1

The Name You Don't Know

In the spring of 1988, Jacqueline Davis sits in her parents' living room, preparing to ask her mother and two aunts an important question. She has big, big dreams for this baby.

"What should I name him?" No one says a word.

"What letter do you want his name to start with?" one aunt finally asks.

"I need a name that starts with a V," Jacqueline quickly says. This is important, after all, since her oldest child is a 4-year-old named Vernon. She hopes that the brothers will be close because they share the same first letter in their names.

"How about Vincent?" one aunt says. "That is such a nice name." Jacqueline shakes her head.

"Victor, or Vic?" the other aunt says. Jacqueline shakes her head again and again. No one says anything for a few minutes until Jacqueline's mother, Adaline, breaks the silence with her first suggestion.

"I've always liked the name Vaughn," Adaline says, looking up with pride. "That sounds nice—Vaughn Davis." Jacqueline does not dismiss the name, but something doesn't feel quite right.

As time passes, the four women realize there are not many options for boy names that start with the letter V. Jacqueline comes up with an idea: she likes the name Dante and decides to combine that with her mom's favorite name.

"How about Vaughn-tay," Jacqueline says.

"Oooh, I like that!" the other women say excitedly.

"How would you spell that?" one aunt asks.

"I don't know," Jacqueline says. "We'll worry about that later."

A few weeks later, on May 27th, Jacqueline rushes to Greater Southeast Community Hospital in Washington, D.C. For a pregnant woman, there are three stages to labor—the process for introducing a baby to the world. Jacqueline needs a few hours in the final stage of labor to deliver her baby boy. After hugging and holding her son, she hands him to a nurse, so he can be cleaned and examined.

"What do you want to name him?" the nurse asks.

"Vaughn-tay," Jacqueline says.

"How would you like to spell that?" the nurse asks.

"I'm not sure. I'll trust you." Jacqueline tells the nurse that the boy's middle name will be Ottis, after his father.

The nurse is from France and spells the name in a way that seems right to her.

Vontée Ottis Davis

In France, the "e" with a mark that points right and upward is called the *aigu* accent. Perhaps the most common French word with the aigu accent is *café*—a small shop that sells drinks and light snacks. The aigu accent is different than the grave accent mark that points left and upward. A common French word with the grave accent is *très*, which means very.

After a few weeks of living with her parents, Jacqueline decides she wants to move in with Otis, Vontée's father. Adaline thinks that is not a good idea. She believes Otis is a negative influence on her daughter and worries that the young couple will not be able to properly take care of Vontée. As Jacqueline grabs her bags, boxes, and baby, Adaline warns her, "Don't expect to come back here."

Jacqueline nods and walks out the front door. She believes she can handle the obstacles ahead of her. Vontée moves into a new home in a different part of Washington D.C., but there will be many more moves ahead for him. There will be unexpected challenges ahead for them all.

Chapter 2

D.C. and Drugs

Washington, D.C. (District of Columbia) has a proud history. Long ago, the country's first president, George Washington, lived at Mt. Vernon: his estate on the banks of the Potomac River in Virginia. In 1790, Congress gave President Washington the authority to pick the capital of the United States. Naturally, he chose 100 square miles near his home, with Virginia and Maryland donating land. This area became known as Washington, D.C.

13

But Washington, D.C.'s proud history faces challenges of its own. A terrible epidemic sweeps through the city. Some of the city's darkest days occur before and during Vontée's childhood. A very addictive drug is introduced into the city. It impacts a lot of other U.S. cities too, but none more than D.C. Since the majority of citizens in the city are African-American, the drug devastates the African-American community.

The drug destroys families, tears apart neighborhoods, and results in many deaths. Murders become common even in areas where families try to live peacefully. D.C. is named the "nation's murder capital." Even D.C.'s mayor, Marion Barry, succumbs to the drug. He is arrested and sentenced to six months in jail. It seems no one is safe from this drug and its effect.

Vontée's parents cannot escape the grip of the drug either.

The drug is dangerous because it is relatively cheap, it's easy to access, and it stimulates the body quickly. This means a user's heart rate increases and they feel a burst of energy. Often the drug causes the widening of the pupils in your eyes. This makes your eyes very sensitive to light and creates blurred vision.

The drug also affects your mind and mood. Some users become violent or unpredictable. They might even experience hallucinations, which are sensations that appear real but are created in the brain. Because addiction happens very quickly, users often focus on ways to get more drugs and start missing their daily responsibilities.

Vontée's parents are known for being fun and kind, but they are very different when the drug is in their bodies. They do not take care of themselves well, and they also do not take care of Vontée, who by now has two younger siblings. That concerns other family members.

Vontée is too young to recognize the problems.

Chapter 3
Grandma Adaline

No one worries more about Vontée and his siblings than Grandma Adaline. She grew up in Nathalie, Virginia, near the North Carolina border, about four hours south of D.C. Nathalie was named after Natalie Otey, the daughter of an important local landowner in the late 1800s.

Adaline's parents lived on a tobacco farm and worked as sharecroppers. That means they lived and worked on land owned by a farmer. In return, her family shared the crops produced on their portion of land. After slavery officially ended in the U.S., sharecropping became an important way for farmers—particularly those in the south—to run their farms.

Tobacco is the main ingredient in cigarettes. Nicotine is one of the chemicals added into cigarettes and is very addictive. Nicotine is a stimulant, which means it makes most people feel like they have more energy. In the U.S., cigarette smoking is the leading preventable cause of death, according to the Centers for Disease Control and Prevention.

Cultivating tobacco is hard work. It's usually hot and humid in the fields. If you

don't handle tobacco properly, it can make you sick. After pulling tobacco from the ground, the large leaves have to be laid on a big table to dry.

Adaline's family lived in a shack, which is a small house that isn't constructed well. They had no electricity, no water, and no bathroom.

Adaline had three brothers and three sisters. But after her mother died of an illness, Adaline and her siblings were split

between different relatives. Three brothers and a sister went to live with different cousins. Another sister went with an aunt and uncle. Adaline and the last sister stayed with their grandmother.

Adaline longed for more than a simple farm life.

"I'm leaving home," Adaline tells her sister and grandmother.

"Why? Where will you go?" her grandmother asks.

"I don't know," Adaline says, "but I can't stay here."

When she is 18 years old, Adaline grabs her bag of belongings and waves goodbye to her family. Her grandmother and sister cry.

Adaline winds up in Washington, D.C., and she lands a job as a nanny. A nanny is someone who has a lot of experience caring for children. She watches three young children while the mom and dad work at their jobs during the day.

Adaline works very hard constantly changing diapers, making meals, reading to the children, playing games, dealing with tantrums, and ending fights. But she grows fond of the children, and she appreciates the work much more than tobacco farming. In her free time, she makes friends, listens to music, and explores the city.

She meets a special man named Lynwood, who is kind and thoughtful. They marry and move into their home in a northwest neighborhood in D.C. Adaline and Lynwood raise six children in the home, and she instills in them one of the core lessons of her life.

Adaline's Rule

"No one can choose your life," Adaline says.

Vontée loves to hear Grandma's story: she is the glue that holds the family together. He is glad that she was brave enough to leave home in search of a new life.

Little Grady Gets Punished

When he is six years old, Vontée likes going to see his dad's mother, Grandma Ganeva. She lives in a heavily wooded area on Old Brand Avenue in Maryland, not too far from the southeast part of D.C.

Grandma Ganeva is what the kids call "old-school." A native of Georgia, she had 12 children, including Vontée's dad, Otis. She was tough and independent with no neighbors close by.

There are usually several cousins at Grandma's, but Vontée likes to play with Janeese and Little Grady, whose father is Big Grady. One of their favorite activities is playing with Grandma's mixed black Labrador named Sheba.

Sheba has a rolled-up rag that is her most prized possession. The kids bother Sheba by taking the rag and playing keep away.

"Over here, over here!" Vontée yells at Little Grady.

Because Sheba is a big dog, Little Grady can't just hold the rag above his head, so he launches it when Sheba comes close. Sometimes, when Sheba gets a hold of the rag, the kids play tug of war with her. It's hard to tell if Sheba enjoys these games or not.

But there's one certainty: the kids will tire before Sheba does. She loves her rag, and she will not stop until it's in her possession.

When the temperature drops, Grandma's house gets awfully cold. That's because she does not have heat in her home. Instead, she uses a fireplace with real wood. There's a large stack of wood near the shed, and she commands the kids to retrieve it.

"Go grab me some wood," Grandma yells at the boys.

They put on their coats and head outside. The wood is stacked three feet high and four feet wide. The boys compete to see who can carry the most firewood and who can deliver it the fastest.

"Ready, set, go!" Little Grady says.

Vontée wins the speed competition, but Little Grady wins the volume competition, carrying five logs at a time.

Grandma has an old fireplace with a metal screen. Vontée really likes to sit near the fire as she lights the logs. He takes a deep whiff as the wood starts to burn, and he smiles as the wood crackles. He marvels at how long the fire runs and fears how hot it gets. The entire process amazes him.

Sometimes, Grandma gives the kids some money to walk a few blocks down the road to the corner store. The cousins usually share so they can each get a piece of candy. But on their second visit, Little Grady is not satisfied with one small piece.

"That's not enough," he says.

He wants fist-sized candy bars and packages full of dozens of gummy bears!

There's always just one clerk at the store. Little Grady coolly walks the aisles, scanning all the junk food and snacks. When the clerk checks a customer out, he stuffs candy into his pants, under his baggy t-shirt, and acts like he hasn't done anything.

The other four cousins can only afford one Atomic FireBall each. They check out with the clerk and walk out of the store. Little Grady is waiting outside with a sly smile on his face. When they are halfway back to Grandma's house, Little Grady pulls up his shirt and reveals two big candy bars and a package of gummy bears.

"Whoa!" one of the cousins says. "Where did you get all that?"

"I took it," Little Grady says.

As they walk back, Little Grady scarfs down all the treats by himself. He's got a tummy ache when they get back to Grandma's, but he certainly does not complain.

A few days later, the cousins return to the candy store. Vontée notices Little Grady walking up and down the aisles. Vontée wonders if he should take some candy too. It sure would taste yummy! But Vontée knows that stealing is wrong. Besides, what if he gets caught? Will the police chase him? Will he go to jail?

Vontée decides he will not steal. He and four other cousins can only afford small lollipops each. Halfway back to Grandma's, Little

Grady shows an even bigger haul: four candy bars, a package of gummy bears, and five lollipops. This time, he offers to share his spoils.

"I'm good," Vontée politely tells Little Grady. "I'm kind of full from lunch."

The third time is not so lucky for Little Grady. On the next trip, while the clerk checks out a customer, the store owner follows him from a distance and watches him sneak candy into the elastic band on his shorts.

"Aha, I caught you!" the store owner says. "I knew you kids were up to no good!"

The store owner does not call the police. Instead, he calls Grandma Ganeva, whom he has known for years. Grandma comes into the store a few times a week to buy coffee and snacks.

"Miss Ganeva, please come to the store," the owner says on the telephone. "I caught one of your nephews stealing candy from me."

When she arrives a few minutes later in her car, Grandma grabs something from the passenger seat. It's a tree branch.

"Oh no, Grandma's got a switch!" one cousin shouts. A switch is what an adult uses to spank a child when they have done something very, very naughty.

When he realizes what is about to happen, Little Grady panics and repeatedly apologizes to his Grandma.

"I'm sorry, Grandma," he desperately says.

"Oh, you're gonna be sorry all right," she replies.

Little Grady tries to defend his behind from the switch, but Grandma moves his hands. She then spanks him hard with the switch three times.

Grandma Ganeva's Rule

"Don't take anything that is not yours," Grandma says as she spanks Little Grady.

Little Grady cries. His bottom hurts, but the shame of stealing and the embarrassment of being punished in front of his cousins is even worse.

"What do you say to Mr. Roberts?" Grandma says, referring to the store owner.

"I'm sorry," Little Grady says between sobs. "I'll never steal from you again."

"That's right!" Grandma says. "And you're going to work to pay him back."

Vontée feels bad Little Grady got in so much trouble, but he is glad he made the right choice and did not steal.

Chapter 5

Something's Not Right

Back at home, Vontée's parents can be nice and caring. The kids brighten up when dad brings home snacks and treats, and they enjoy mom's jokes with her big laugh and smile.

But this isn't normal.

The truth is, mom and dad are very unpredictable. One moment Mom warmly hugs one of the children, and the next moment she storms out of their two-bedroom apartment and disappears for hours or days at a time. One minute Dad is watching television, and the next he is screaming at whomever is closest to him.

Their behavior confuses the kids, especially Vontée since he is the oldest in their apartment. Vontée is just six years old and he must take care of his younger siblings, Michael and Ebony. He learns to prepare formula and

change diapers. And though it's not safe for a child his age, he also learns how to use the microwave and the stove.

This is Vontée's normal.

He looks after his little brother and sister because his parents are rarely home. And when they are, they often fight and yell at each other. Sometimes, the kids hear things breaking and slamming against walls. This scares Michael and Ebony, so they crawl into bed with Vontée until all the noise stops—or until they fall asleep.

One autumn day, Vontée is on the playground at school when he hears someone shouting in the distance. As the person gets closer, the sound gets more recognizable.

Vontée freezes. It's his mom's voice!

Mom runs toward Vontée, but there is a fence around the playground.

"Mom, what are you doing here?" Vontée asks quietly.

"What do you mean?" Mom coldly responds. "I'm a grown-up; I do what I want!"

"Is something wrong?" Vontée asks.

"No, I just felt like seeing you. That all right with you?" Mom asks, attitude dripping from her voice.

"Look, I'm gonna finish playing with my friends before recess ends," Vontée says, whirling around toward the swings.

Really, though, Vontée feels embarrassed. None of his friends' parents show up shouting during recess. They check in at the office and get escorted by someone who works at the school.

Things start to get worse. As Vontée approaches his friends, his mom roars even more.

"Don't you walk away from me!" she yells. "Who do you think you are?"

Vontée's mom includes a few bad words—words that are not allowed to be spoken, written, or even thought of at school. Instead of stopping at the swing set, Vontée runs toward the school entrance.

Now he feels something different. He later learns the proper word: *humiliation*.

Vontée's mom's visit is the talk of the school for two days. Kids make fun of his mom, and they also make fun of his name.

"What's up with your name? It's so weird. Who has ever heard of anyone named Von-tee," Johnny says, mispronouncing the name.

Vontée defends himself. "My name rhymes with *say*, not *see*," Vontée says. "Get it right!"

Later that night, Vontée makes a decision. He stops spelling his name V-o-n-t-é-e and starts spelling his name V-o-n-t-a-e.

None of his teachers protest; they are sympathetic of his challenges. Vontae is thankful that his friends at school stick by him.

"I think Vontae is a really cool name," one of his friends says after lunch. "You're the only Vontae I know!"

Grandpa Saves Vontae

Grandma Adaline is the family's rock. Everyone can count on her for encouragement or an honest talk. She unconditionally loves her family, especially her grandchildren. Grandpa Lynwood is quiet and strong. His grandchildren are often afraid of him. If you are horsing around, you stop when Grandpa steps into the room.

One Saturday afternoon, three older cousins snatch one of Vontae's toys from him and play "keep away." When they hear Grandpa's footsteps coming down the stairs, one of the cousins catches the action figure and immediately shoves it into Vontae's chest.

"Here, take it and stop whining, or you're going to get us all in trouble!" the cousin says.

Grandpa's voice strikes fear in children. If you really upset him, he lifts you up—like a bear picks up a cub—and glares deep into your eyes like he is looking straight through you. That means you are in *serious* trouble!

But Grandpa has a soft side too. He tends to the children when they are sick, wiping drippy noses, running warm baths, and placing Band-Aids on scrapes. When the grandkids sleep over on some Friday nights, Grandpa wakes up very early, heads to

McDonald's and returns to the house with egg sandwiches for everyone. This is a big treat!

Grandpa is also generous in letting the kids have candy; his favorites are Reese's Peanut Butter Cups and Jolly Ranchers. Grandpa lets Vontae have a Jolly Rancher when he is seven years old. Vontae excitedly twists the wrapper off. He pops the candy into his mouth and sucks on the sweet treat. But as he is enjoying it, Vontae starts to choke because the hard candy slips down his throat.

Vontae gags; he cannot breathe. He lifts his hands toward his throat. He is afraid.

Grandpa calmly gets off his bed and kneels down on the ground behind Vontae so their heads are close. Then Grandpa lifts up Vontae's elbows, places his left thumb just above Vontae's belly button, and locks his right hand around his left hand.

"This is the Heimlich Maneuver," Grandpa tells Vontae. "This should help us get that candy out of your mouth."

The Heimlich Maneuver is named after Dr. Henry Heimlich, who first described the technique to help people who are choking. When it is done properly, the Heimlich Maneuver assists in removing objects that are blocking a victim's airway.

With Vontae securely wrapped in his arms, Grandpa makes a fist and places it below the center of Vontae's abdomen. He thrusts his fist up and in. After three pumps, the Jolly Rancher flies out of Vontae's mouth, across the bedroom, and lands on Grandpa's beige-colored carpet.

"Are you all right?" Grandpa asks Vontae.

Vontae takes several deep breaths. He is no longer afraid. Grandpa saved his life.

"Thank you, Grandpa!" Vontae says. He wraps his arms around his Grandpa's neck to give him a warm hug.

A few minutes later, after Vontae settles down, Grandpa sits him on the end of his bed.

Grandpa's Rule
"When something bad happens, stay calm and do not panic."

Vontae nods his head and races downstairs. He can't wait to tell everyone that Grandpa is a hero!

Chapter 7

Pranks with Princess

Vontae grows up fast. He doesn't have a choice since he must take care of his younger siblings at home. When he is four, five, and six years old, Vontae is much more serious than other children his age.

But one person starts to get him to loosen up—his sister Veronica, who is 13 months younger than he is. Everyone calls her Princess, and she likes to have fun. Vontae and Princess are always joking and playing tricks on each other.

"Princess, you got something on your shirt," Vontae says to Princess, pointing his right index finger toward her chest. When Princess looks down, Vontae runs his finger up her face.

"Made you look!" he teases.

Princess then chases Vontae all over the house until they both quit because they're either laughing too hard or they are too tired to keep running.

They do other things to mess with each other. There's *Distract and Snatch*, where one gets the attention of the other and then takes away a toy or treat. There's *Oops, Did I Do That?* when someone—usually Vontae—spills water on the other and insists that it was an accident.

One of their biggest competitions is racing to get a seat at dinner time. Their grandparents' kitchen is small, so the table only has four seats. When Grandma calls everyone to dinner, the children sprint to get a seat. Usually, there are only two seats available since Grandpa and Grandma always have a place.

If you don't get a seat, you have to sit at the top of the basement steps.

Princess and Vontae look out for each other. Vontae thinks his grandparents always give Princess what she wants, so he pushes her to ask for things that he really wants.

"Ask them for a Snickers bar, Princess," Vontae whispers.

"They'll let you have one. Then you and I can split it!"

Without fail, Princess tries to please her brother. Vontae takes his sister's trust in him seriously.

During a Sunday dinner, Princess is smacking her lips, really enjoying some of Grandma's baked chicken. Others are looking at Princess because of her noise. It's only a matter of time before Grandma firmly reminds Princess about table manners. It's not considered polite to eat with your elbows on the table, talk with your mouth full, or smack your lips while chewing.

Vontae speaks softly. "Look Princess," he says, stabbing a piece of chicken with his fork. "I chew with my mouth closed." Vontae places the bite-sized piece of chicken in his mouth. He does not speak as he carefully chews it up and swallows.

Vontae smiles at his sister.

Princess pauses and then realizes the subtle message her brother is communicating. She chews much quicker and louder than Vontae. She then looks at how Grandma and Grandpa are eating; they aren't making much noise at all.

For the rest of dinner, Princess slows down, quietly eating her food and keeping her mouth shut.

Chapter 8

Vontae Throws a Tantrum

Grandma and Grandpa do not make a lot of money. Grandma cleans houses and Grandpa cleans schools. They have a weekly budget to make sure they don't spend money they do not have. This means Grandma and Grandpa must be careful not to buy too much when they go to the store. To save money, they clip coupons, which are small, printed pieces of paper with a discount on products.

Vontae likes going to the store with his grandparents. It always feels like a special trip! His favorite store is Shoppers Food Warehouse because they always have the largest packages of his top foods.

On one trip, when he is eight years old, Vontae pushes the cart as his grandparents walk through the store.

39

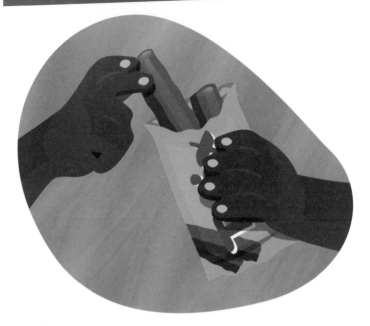

As they turn into an aisle, Vontae sees the gold packaging of a treat he loves. It's called Twix, a chocolate bar topped with sticky, yummy caramel.

"Can I have one?" Vontae asks his Grandpa. "They are so good!"

Grandpa, who is holding the grocery list, shakes his head. "No, we don't have extra money for candy."

Vontae thinks for a moment. He pictures pulling out a bar and biting into the chocolatey-caramel biscuit of goodness. *What can I say to make this delicious dream a reality?* He thinks he knows what he did wrong.

"Please, can I have a Twix?" Vontae asks in his sweetest voice possible.

Grandpa shakes his head again. "If I buy you a candy," he says, "then I have to buy everyone a candy. The answer is no."

Vontae stops pushing the cart. He dramatically falls to the floor, wildly flails his arms, and cries loudly. In one seamless motion, Grandpa takes control of the shopping cart and follows Grandma down an aisle. In the middle of his fit, with his eyes closed, Vontae does not see them walk away.

He hopes they will give in and give him what he wants. But he mostly expects they will yell at him, pull him up, and drag him along as they continue shopping.

They don't do either. They simply let him have a tantrum.

After a few moments, Vontae realizes no one is reacting. Not only have his grandparents moved on, other shoppers also walk past him without looking at him.

Vontae feels silly.

He bounces up onto his feet and quickly catches up to his grandparents. He does not dare say anything for the remainder of the shopping trip, thinking maybe—just maybe—they will forget the whole episode even happened.

No one says anything as they leave the store or even as they arrive at Grandma and Grandpa's house. But after they unpack the groceries, Grandpa calls Vontae into the living room.

Grandpa's Rule

"Acting up doesn't get you what you want," he says.

Grandpa makes a promise to Vontae. "Behaving that way will never work in this house," he says. "Don't you try that mess again."

Vontae nods his head in agreement.

Chapter 9

Avoiding Ronnie

Vontae's neighborhood is dangerous, overrun with drug dealers and drug users, including his parents. Most of the drug dealers belong to gangs—an organized group of criminals. They buy large quantities of illegal drugs, and then they sell those drugs at much higher prices.

In a big city like Washington, D.C., there are lots of gangs that compete with each other and break laws to make money and grow in power. Gangs even use kids Vontae's age to help them. Because they don't look threatening, little boys serve as lookouts, which means they warn the gang members when police are nearby. If a lookout sees a police officer, they make a noise, like a special whistle, or a gesture to give the gang members a heads up that they could be in trouble.

Lookouts receive candy, snacks, cash, or even fancy sneakers for doing a good job.

In Vontae's neighborhood, most of the kids are not raised by both of their parents, and all of them know someone in their family who is involved in selling or using drugs. In D.C., drugs are a major problem, and dealers often stick out with their designer jeans, sweat suits, flashy necklaces, and colorful cars with loud sound systems.

Even as an elementary school student, Vontae knows he does not want to be in a gang or do anything related to drugs. He sees how drugs impact his parents, which frightens him. Those influences also scare Grandma. This is why she reminds Vontae to think about the kind of people he hangs out with.

Grandma's Rule
"Choose your friends wisely," Grandma says.

One of Vontae's best friends is Joe. After school, they play pickup basketball or head to Joe's house to play with action figures or watch TV. Vontae feels safe there because Joe's mom stays at home, and she is very nice.

Vontae also likes going there because he gets to eat Joe's favorite snack.

Joe pulls an orange package out of a cabinet, dumps the dried noodles and a packet of flavoring into a bowl, adds some water, and puts it in the microwave for a few minutes. When the bowl is steaming, Joe puts two slices of cheese on top and microwaves everything for another 20 seconds.

Joe's eyes light up when his snack is ready.

"Yum, Oodles of Noodles," Joe says. "Want to try some?"

Vontae nods. He doesn't know about this snack, but he is kind of hungry. It's been a long time since the free lunch at school. He grabs a fork and spins some of the soft, hot noodles onto it. He blows on the fork a few times then opens his mouth and takes a bite.

"Hey, this is good!"

Joe insists Vontae takes the bowl and he makes another. Joe is happy that Vontae loves his favorite after-school snack. When Joe's bowl is ready, the boys head to the TV and watch Tom

& Jerry, a silly cartoon about a cat and mouse that are always trying to bother each other.

Vontae and Joe sometimes hang out with another friend named Jason. They try to avoid one boy in the neighborhood named Ronnie.

There are lots of stories about Ronnie—and none of them are good. He skips school, he steals cars, and he damages vehicles, public benches, and bus stops. Vontae and Joe try to stay away from Ronnie, but Ronnie is their age, and he wants them to hang out.

As they walk toward Joe's house one afternoon, Ronnie asks them to slow down so he can catch up.

"Hey, let's go have some fun," Ronnie says. "I've got something cool in my bag."

Vontae and Joe are nervous. But before they can even say no, Ronnie rips open his backpack and reveals two cartons of eggs.

"We're going to throw these at the Metro buses!" Ronnie says with gusto, like it is the greatest idea ever. But Vontae and Joe know it is not. Still, Ronnie kind of scares  them, and he is always asking them to hang out.

Vontae thinks, *Well, at least he's not asking me to help him steal a car.*

Ronnie waves for them to follow him. Vontae feels a tingly sensation in his tummy. Deep down, he knows this is wrong.

"Come on, it's a lot of fun," Ronnie pleads.

Vontae and Joe decide to tag along. They jog a block, and Ronnie ducks behind a large bush just off the main road. A bus comes by there every eight or nine minutes.

When the first bus comes rumbling toward them, Ronnie steps out and hurls two raw eggs one right after the other. One 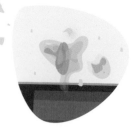 startles a passenger inside as it splats on the window facing them. The other nearly hits the American flag just outside where the bus driver sits.

Ronnie erupts in laughter. "Now you guys try!" he says.

Vontae and Joe exchange looks. Neither of them wants to, but they have come this far. What will happen if they tell Ronnie no now?

After a few minutes, Vontae and Joe grab an egg for each hand. As a bus nears them, they both step out and each toss the eggs. Despite the size of the big, public bus, Vontae and Joe each miss with one egg, but their second attempts hit the target. A passenger gives the boys a dirty look, as the egg explodes on the window.

Ronnie breaks into laughter again. Vontae and Joe do not. They duck back behind the bush and uncomfortably fake a laugh.

"Isn't this great?" Ronnie asks.

Vontae feels the opposite of great; in fact, he feels regret.

Joe looks at Vontae, shifts his eyes, and tips his head in the other direction. "Well, I better get home before my mom freaks out," Joe says. "Vontae, she's expecting you too."

Vontae nods. "Oh yeah," he quickly says, "we better get going."

But Ronnie is not done.

"Come on! I still have 18 eggs left," Ronnie protests. "What am I going to do with them all?"

As they start to walk away, Vontae says, "Maybe you can make a few omelets."

When the boys get to Joe's house, they start their routine and prepare their Oodles of Noodles.

"You're later than usual," Joe's mom says. "Everything OK?"

The boys pretend not to hear her. Something feels off to both of them. The snack doesn't taste quite as good, and the cartoons are not so funny.

"We shouldn't have done that," Vontae quietly says to Joe.

"We are lucky we didn't get caught," Joe responds. "What should we do?"

The boys talk some more then head to the kitchen.

"Mom, Vontae and I were late for a reason," he says, his head low.

Joe's mom is concerned as she hears the story, but she does not punish the boys. Instead, she hugs Joe.

"I'm glad you're OK," she says, "and I hope you learned a lesson. You know the difference between right and wrong."

When he gets home, Vontae wants to confess to his parents too. But, like most times, neither of them is home. Instead, he transitions into his routine of caring for his younger siblings and getting dinner ready.

Chapter 10

Vernon Plays Ball

Vontae wants to play organized sports, but he is too young. His big brother Vernon, though, is ready. Vernon usually stays with Grandma and Grandpa, so he asks them to fill out and sign a form that will let him play tackle football.

"Oh no," Grandma says, furiously shaking her head. "Football is dangerous. Duke, I don't want you to get hurt!" (Duke is Vernon's nickname, and Grandma calls him that more than anyone else.)

Grandpa likes football and watches Washington's professional team. But Grandma never pays attention and only hears how football players get hurt a lot. Even though they wear helmets, the players sometimes hurt their heads.

Vernon does not know much about football either. But he likes to be active and outside. Besides, he is athletic. He rides a skateboard and does a few tricks. He can run fast and does back flips off the monkey bars. None of his friends can keep up with him!

A lot of boys sign up for football, and Vernon does not want to miss out on the fun.

"Grandma, I just want to hang out with my friends," Vernon says. "It's no big deal."

Grandma still does not like football, but she decides to change her mind. She signs Vernon's paper.

"I'm not taking you to a hospital!" she says as she hands the paper back.

Vernon does not know what to wear to football. Some of the boys have on cleats, which are shoes with hard pieces of plastic called "studs" on the bottom. The studs give the wearer extra traction on the field so they can avoid slipping. Vernon cannot afford cleats, so he just wears his regular sneakers.

One of the volunteer coaches tells the players to line up.

"My name is Coach Malik, and these are my assistants, Gary and Big Hank. How many of you have played organized football before?"

Everyone raises their hands except Vernon and one other boy. The three coaches then go down the line and ask each boy what position he plays. Vernon, toward the middle, hears three positions the most: quarterback, running back, and receiver. When a coach reaches him, Vernon is speechless.

"What position do you play?" Big Hank asks.

"I don't know," Vernon whispers.

"No big deal," Big Hank says. "We'll find the right spot for you. But you're so big, I'm thinking you can be one of my linemen!"

That is the truth. Vernon is the second-biggest player on the field. But he does not want to be a lineman. He wants to have the ball in his hand, like everyone else.

"Now let's line up and see what we're working with," Coach Malik says. "Race from this sideline to the other sideline."

All the boys line up and get low, into a sprinting position. Coach Malik blows his whistle. Vernon panics; he was not ready for such an abrupt start. He falls behind. But he runs as hard as he can. He quickly makes up ground. Halfway across the field, he takes a slight lead. At the other sideline, Vernon crosses first—by a wide margin. The coaches cannot believe their eyes. Despite his size, Vernon is the fastest player.

"All right," Coach Malik says. "Get a quick drink of water and let's try that again!"

As he gets some water, Vernon overhears two other boys talking.

"There's no way that big kid is faster than me! He probably cheated and started early."

This makes Vernon mad. He is determined to win the race again. Coach Malik calls on the boys to line up, waits a moment, then loudly blows his whistle. All the boys seem to run even harder and faster, but Vernon still reaches the other sideline first, well ahead of everyone else.

In other drills, Vernon looks uncomfortable and awkward, which is not surprising since he has never learned how to play football or even practiced the sport. But when he has the ball in his hands, Vernon is unstoppable because the defenders can't catch him or tackle him to the ground.

Afterwards, as he grabs his water bottle to leave, Vernon sees Big Hank walking toward him.

"The bad news is, I won't get to work with you as a lineman, and you have a lot to learn," Big Hank says. "The good news is, you will be our fullback and the focus of our offense."

Vernon smiles. By now he knows what this means—the ball will be in his hands a lot!

chapter 11

Standing Up to Dad

Vontae feels like he lives in two different worlds. There is order at school: each day starts at 8 a.m., there are two periods before lunch and recess, more classes after that, and dismissal at 2:50 p.m. He goes to the same classes, hangs out with the same friends, plays the same games after lunch, and learns from the same teachers. There is mostly calm and consistency at school.

But there is mostly chaos and unsteadiness at home.

Vontae never knows which parent will be home; often, neither mom nor dad are around, and there are never any notes communicating when they will return. He frequently arrives home to find the front or back door wide open and fears someone broke in.

Sometimes, if Mom is home, she asks about his day and makes a snack for the kids while they watch cartoons together. Other times, Mom ignores them, or, even worse, blames them for things they do not understand.

Dad is not around as much, but his presence usually ignites arguments and fights with Mom. The other kids know the drill: when voices get loud, they find Vontae, run to their bedroom, and hide in the corner furthest from the door. They don't talk. Instead, they wait until the voices quiet down, or they hear police sirens (Mom calls the police a lot). Most often, they hear a pair of feet scurry across the apartment, then the front door opens and slams shut.

It's confusing at home.

The kids will never forget their scariest night. Their parents yell louder than usual, and they hear objects crashing and chairs

slamming against the wall. The kids assume their usual positions, hiding in the bedroom. But this time, Vontae's brother and sister are so afraid that they are crying.

Loudly.

Vontae tries to settle them down, but the turmoil persists in the living room. The minutes feel like months, and anger starts to build in Vontae. His dad is doing most of the screaming because Mom is crying.

Vontae wants his parents to stop fighting, but more than anything, he wants his brother and sister to stop crying. He decides he cannot stay in the bedroom any longer, so he stands up and marches into the living room.

With his meanest look, Vontae glares at his dad.

"Stop fighting with Mom! You're scaring Ebony and Michael!"

Vontae is full of fear, but he tries to be brave and look strong. He holds his breath; Dad's eyes are filled with rage.

Dad stands still for a moment. His attitude suddenly changes. Then, without saying a word, he turns and walks toward the back door. He quickly opens it and walks out, quietly closing it behind him.

The apartment is quiet for the first time in 35 minutes. Mom's loud cry changes into a sob, as she remains balled up on the floor. Vontae runs back into the bedroom and hugs his siblings.

"We're all OK now," he whispers quietly to them. "Let's go lay down and get some sleep."

Vontae holds each of their hands and leads them toward his bed. Exhausted and emotionally drained, all three kids fall asleep within 15 minutes, laying beside each other.

Who knows what tomorrow will bring?

Chapter 12

Not Like Dad

Vontae struggles, but he tries to get himself and his siblings in bed by 8 p.m. Most of the time, Michael and Ebony listen to their big brother. But they resist more around bed time. Vontae tells them to stop whatever it is they are doing. Then he instructs them to begin their nighttime routine: clean themselves up, put on pajamas, and brush their teeth.

This, of course, takes a while, which is why Vontae usually begins the process at around 7:15 p.m. Bed time is when Vontae appreciates having Mom or Dad around the most. They are helpful getting Michael and Ebony into bed because everyone agrees the kids need rest.

One spring evening, Vontae has no trouble getting Michael and Ebony ready for bed. All three kids are in their beds by 8 p.m. About 10 minutes later, before anyone is asleep, they hear a commotion toward the rear of the apartment. Vontae bolts from the bedroom and peeks toward the back door. Dad staggers in with two white plastic bags of food.

Something doesn't look right though. Vontae notices dark red splatters on the white bags. His eyes shift and he sees more red on his dad's jeans and yellow shirt.

Dad is bleeding. A lot. He slams the back door shut, locks the main handle, and even turns the deadbolt further up. He drops the grocery bags, and a split second later, collapses on the white linoleum floor.

Vontae knows something is wrong. Within a minute, he hears a bang at the back door.

"We're gonna get you!" a deep voice yells.

Vontae hears the voices of at least two more men, and they slam into the door with such force it shakes. Dad gets up, and leans his shoulder into the door, as if trying to keep it in place. Another crash sounds at the door. This time, Vontae hears wood starting to splinter.

Dad runs toward the stove and grabs a frying pan.

Vontae has seen enough. He knows the corner of the bedroom isn't safe, not with hulking strangers trying to break down their back door. He sprints to the bedroom and motions to Ebony and Michael to follow him.

"We need to get out of here!"

Michael and Ebony do not protest. They hop up and head toward the front door.

They run out the door, down the stairs, and Vontae bangs on Ms. Johnson's front door. She is the nicest of the neighbors: the one who smiles at them and speaks to them. She opens the door right away, as if she expects the children's arrival.

"Come on in," Ms. Johnson says.

She opens and closes the door fast. No one says a word. Ebony softly cries as Ms. Johnson comforts her with a hug.

Within minutes, Vontae hears the wail of police cruisers. By this time, he can tell the difference between fire sirens and

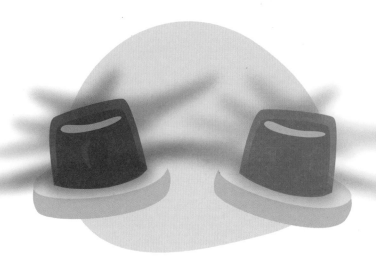

police sirens. Fire engines sound more like air raid horns with a continuous deeper, longer sound. Police and ambulance often use noises in bursts that are more like a "wail" or "yelp."

Vontae's dad may end up being taken away by police in handcuffs again. Or he may end up leaving in an ambulance since he was bleeding. But Vontae is thankful that order will be restored at home.

There is more chaos and more confusion.

Vontae makes a decision while waiting in Ms. Johnson's living room. *I will not be like my dad,* he thinks.

Vontae wants to create order at home.

Chapter 13

Hoops with Carl

In fifth grade, Vontae tries Pee Wee football for the first time. Any fifth grader can play, as long as they are under 125 pounds. That eliminates a few of Vontae's bigger classmates at school, but the adults make the rule to try and protect smaller boys.

The first practice is at a Boys & Girls Club. The coaches run the kids through drills and games. Vontae does not enjoy himself.

"This isn't as much fun as basketball!" Vontae tells his friend Carl.

The truth is, Vontae does not like football as much because he is not as confident playing this sport. Dribbling comes naturally to him, and he quickly learns to shoot, pass, and play defense.

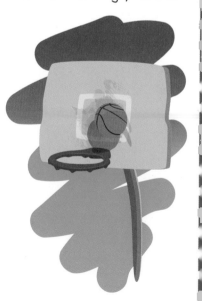

A few of the others snicker when Vontae attempts to throw a football, and he sometimes drops the passes thrown to him.

Vontae goes to football practices and games. But

whenever he can, he wants to play basketball—and Carl is always up for hoops. Carl does not mind if they just shoot the ball, play one-on-one games to 21 points, or play pickup with other neighborhood kids. Carl just likes to play. He has game, but so does Vontae.

In their first one-on-one battle, Vontae wins 21–19. Carl wins the next one 21–17. Both are very competitive, and they do not like to lose. They play physically but are most physical when defending each other. Sometimes, they need to take a few minutes away from each other to cool off.

After a while, Vontae and Carl discover they have a lot in common. Well, at least the two most important things: a shared passion for basketball and video games! They decide they will only play together on the same team.

At their school, Truesdell, Carl and Vontae are the two best players, and most of the games are two-on-two. They never lose. The dynamic duo steamroll everyone. The only player who can come close to giving them a game is their friend, A.T.

Vontae and Carl even walk to other neighborhoods to face other boys. But their friendship is about more than basketball. Because they are always together, Vontae and Carl also make sure to look out for one another. Unfortunately, around where they live, there are several gangs, and they are aggressive in recruiting boys their age to join.

Vontae is grateful that Carl is with him at one park they are not familiar with. After they win a game, a bearded guy with a bright jacket walks up to Vontae.

"Hey little man," the guy coolly says, "you got some game. You want to roll with me and my crew?"

Before Vontae has a chance to respond, Carl grabs him by the shoulder and starts to pull him in the opposite direction.

"Vontae, we lost track of time," Carl says. "We need to get home or else I'll get in trouble with my mom."

Vontae does not say a word. He obediently follows his friend's lead. The guy in the bright jacket does not follow them.

After a 20-minute walk, the boys return to Carl's house for a snack and video games.

Chapter 14

Vernon Goes to Dunbar

Seventh and eighth grade start the same way. Vernon stands at a crossroad. One path is positive, filled with hope and a future. The other path is negative, filled with trouble and despair. Though he has potential in school and sports, Vernon is stubborn, and he wants to do what he wants to do. This often means staying out very late and being mischievous. He and his friends go where they please, when they please. He constantly tests the limit of the adults in his life, as well as the police. His actions could land him in serious trouble.

Vernon remembers one evening running with his crew that haunts him.

They walk down a major road in their neighborhood and hear a commotion. It's someone's voice—and it sounds familiar.

"Let's go the other direction," Vernon says.

"Nah, man," Vic replies. "We gotta see what's up."

Vic, E, and Mo keep walking toward the noise. The person is speaking erratically and quickly, not making any sense. As they turn the corner, Vernon is overwhelmed by an unsettling feeling. He *knows* the voice.

"Yo," Maurice says, "that's your mom!"

Vernon's shoulders slump; he debates what to do. His mother

is clearly high on drugs. Because of his embarrassment, Vernon wants to sprint in the opposite direction, running as far away as possible. But instinct kicks in, and he wants to help his mother get to safety.

"Mom," Vernon says gently, "let's get you back home."

Vernon reaches for his mom, but she pulls away.

"Boy, get your hands off me!" she screams at him. "I am just fine. Mind your own business."

With that, she starts to run toward the alley of an apartment building nearby. Vernon could catch her, but he decides not to.

Days later, as he reflects on his life, Vernon comes to a conclusion. He does not want to be like his mom or many others around him who have dim futures. Within weeks, one friend is arrested, another wounded by gunshot. It pains him to see their hurt, their struggles, and their mistakes.

"I've got to get my act together," Vernon says to himself. And it's not just about him. Vernon knows Vontae and his other brothers and sisters are closely watching him.

If they bother going to school, most of the kids Vernon hangs out with head to Roosevelt High. Vernon decides to go to a different school. He hopes to attend Dunbar High School, named after the famous African-American poet, Paul Laurence Dunbar.

The D.C. school is historic, dating back to 1891, because it's one of the first in the United States to educate African-American students. Even into the 1950s, Virginia had no junior high or middle school for African-Americans. D.C. provides a few of the only options in the area. Dunbar High School proudly produces scholars and leaders and boasts one of the first African-American graduates of Harvard University as its principal.

At Dunbar, college is not an option; it's is an expectation.

Vernon knows playing for the football team will help him excel at Dunbar. An hour before the football team's first fall practice, he marches into the office of head football coach, Craig Jefferies.

"I want to play on your team, Coach," Vernon says, handing him a physical and consent form signed by his grandma.

Coach Jefferies thinks someone is playing a joke on him; he had just been telling his assistant coaches that they were a tight end and defensive end away from having a solid team. With his natural size, Vernon immediately fills that need.

This is only the beginning.

Wearing his own workout clothes, Vernon heads toward the field so the coaches can gauge his athleticism and fitness. They ask him to join the other players in running a mile and 400-meter dash. The Dunbar players have already been through offseason conditioning, so they are ready for these final tests.

Vernon, without any formal preseason work, outshines them all.

TOUCHDOWN!

"Look at him," Coach Jefferies says to an assistant as the players run the 400. "He's just smoking everyone out there!"

Vernon quickly establishes himself on the football team, and Vontae makes sure to attend each of his big brother's games.

None is bigger than the Turkey Bowl.

There's no state tournament in D.C., so the Turkey Bowl is essentially the high school championship. For many years, the top east side team played the top west side team in D.C., at Eastern Senior High School. Close to 10,000 fans pack the stadium. There's a Battle of the Bands, which features beautifully arranged programs by talented high school bands.

The D.C. mayor always attends the Turkey Bowl and the major news outlets send at least one reporter.

Vontae looks up to his big brother, but he respects him even more after he witnesses the excitement around the Turkey Bowl.

Vernon worries about Vontae. He hears his little brother

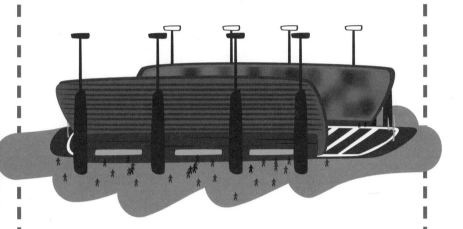

is starting to disobey teachers at school and he sometimes questions Grandpa.

Vernon's Rule

"Don't make the same mistakes I made," Vernon tells Vontae. "You may not be as lucky to avoid serious trouble."

Vontae has gotten in a little trouble at school and at home. But he is afraid to see what big trouble looks like and he takes Vernon's warning to heart.

Vontae decides he needs to make better decisions too.

Chapter 15

Bus Rides

Grandma constantly fears for the safety and well-being of Vontae and his younger siblings.

She lives in the Northwest part of D.C., while Vontae lives in the Southeast. At least once a week, Grandma cooks food at her house, and then asks Aunt Missy to drive her to deliver the food for Vontae, Michael, and Ebony.. Because the city streets are so busy, the ride usually takes Grandma 35 minutes.

Grandma suspects her grandchildren may need more supervision but a phone call confirms the seriousness of the problem. She receives the call early one evening. As soon as she picks up, Vontae starts to speak anxiously without even saying hello.

"My mom isn't home, and I think Ebony is crying because she's hungry. What do I do?" Vontae asks.

Grandma remembers where the powdered milk is, and she calmly instructs Vontae on how to feed his little sister. First, she tells him to wash his hands for 30 seconds with soap and water. She counts the final 10 seconds down as Vontae grows impatient. She instructs him to warm up water on the stovetop—something he already knows how to do—then tells him how much powder and warm water to put in the bottle.

"Make sure the cap is on the bottle and shake it hard," Grandma tells Vontae. "If it looks mixed well, then take the cap off, and test a drop on the inside of your wrist to make sure it's not too hot for her."

Vontae appreciates the calmness in Grandma's voice. He knows she was the right person to call.

"Thanks Grandma," Vontae says.

Because she does not work and support herself, Vontae's mom relies on welfare, a government program that provides money to individuals and families so they can buy food and pay rent. Vontae and his siblings usually have some food at home, but their parents are not always home to prepare meals. Often, Vontae and Michael eat cereal for dinner. Vontae's favorites are Fruit Loops and Frosted Flakes. Sometimes, though, the kids miss meals because there's nothing to eat.

Grandma wants her grandbabies to have home-cooked meals, which is why she drops off meals at least once a week. Sometimes she bakes chicken or makes turkey dishes, along with potato salad. Though he's in elementary school, Vontae knows how to use the microwave, stove, and even the oven. One of Vontae's favorite meals from Grandma is her pot pies.

"I don't know how Vontae does it," Grandma says to Aunt Missy while driving back home late one night. "He has had to grow up way too fast."

Vontae and Michael attend a school near their home in Southeast D.C., but problems start to arise at their school. There is a lot of bullying and gangs are ramping up efforts to recruit new, young members.

Grandma decides they need a new school, but she cannot find any better options near their home. So, she decides to have them switch to a school near her house in Northwest D.C. There's just one problem: how will the boys get there every day?

No one can pick them up each morning and fight traffic to drive the boys to Northwest D.C. Grandma has to make a hard decision: Vontae and Michael will need to ride the city bus each morning and afternoon.

There is no official age when kids can ride the bus alone. Vontae is 10 years old when he starts to take the bus, and he is not the least bit afraid. In Washington D.C., the public buses typically have lots of people riding them. Besides, Vontae is always with Michael.

Grandma gives Vontae all the bus tokens he will need for the week. He makes sure to get Michael up at 6 a.m., so they can walk a block to catch their No. 70 Metrobus toward Grandma's. He gets a rush of excitement when the white bus with red stripes pulls up toward them. It's almost always right on time.

About halfway through their journey, they have to get off and wait for a different bus. Because it's such a busy time for people going to work, they never have to wait more than a couple of minutes. In all, the bus ride adventure takes 25 to 30 minutes.

They get off the second bus along Georgia Avenue, then walk two blocks to Grandma's house. If they didn't have time to eat at home, she feeds them a quick breakfast. After that, Grandma drives them to school.

Vontae and Michael don't mind the bus rides. As the big brother, Vontae gets to pick the seat, and he always wants the one next to the window. He likes to look out and see all the buildings, faces, and cars. Vontae wonders where all the people are going. They look so busy and they're often in a hurry!

Vontae feels that way sometimes too, but he feels peaceful on the bus rides, especially with Michael sitting right next to him.

Chapter 16

Grandma Adaline Takes In Kids

Mom and Dad never really communicate house rules to Vontae, Michael, and Ebony. But there is one.

"If someone knocks on the door," Mom always says, "do not open it!"

Many parents tell that to their children. But Vontae's Mom mostly worries about people who work for CFSA.

Vontae does not know what CFSA means. It stands for Child and Family Services Agency, which D.C. counts on to protect children. The agency's goal is to help children who may be abused or neglected—those who are not receiving the care they need. The agency has a team of social workers who investigate tips from people who are concerned that a child may be in trouble. Perhaps a teacher at school notices a child who regularly comes to school hungry. Or a doctor notices injuries on a child's body during an exam. Maybe a neighbor frequently hears an adult yelling and children crying or screaming.

Vontae's Mom sees CFSA social workers as the enemy.

"Don't ask who it is or nothing!" Mom adds.

One summer day, Ebony crawls out the back door and heads toward the street. Moments later, Vontae races outside and stops her before she gets to the sidewalk. But a policeman notices it all.

He gently bends down and picks up Ebony, who only has a diaper on. The policeman turns to Vontae.

"Is your momma home?" he asks.

Vontae freezes up. Mom is not inside. Neither is his dad. He does not know what to say, so he remains silent.

The policeman is suspicious, but he does not press Vontae. Instead, with Ebony cradled in his arm, he heads to his police cruiser to talk to his partner and then speaks into his radio.

Vontae cannot hear anything he is saying. More time passes, and Michael joins his brother outside. He asks lots of questions, but Vontae does not have answers.

The policeman patiently waits with the boys and holds Ebony. About 30 minutes pass, although Vontae feels like it has been hours. Another vehicle pulls up and Vontae gets nervous. The car has the letters his mom does not like: CFSA.

A woman with a clipboard gets out and speaks to the policeman. Then she approaches Vontae and kindly asks him if she can talk to him.

Vontae does not want to, but he feels he may not have a choice. He tries to answer her questions, but he does not want to upset his mom.

Later, Grandma receives a phone call and learns all that's happened. She discovers CFSA has gotten several calls from neighbors and that social workers have made a number of wellness checks on Vontae, Michael, and Ebony, but no one ever seems to be home when they stop by.

Based on those calls, and Ebony wandering out of the house without any clothes on and without adult supervision, the social worker decides that the children are at high risk.

CFSA wants to remove the children from the home and place them in foster care. That means the children will no longer stay with their mom and dad and they will be placed under the care of CFSA-certified adults either in their private residences or what's called group homes.

There is a strong chance Vontae, Michael, and Ebony will not stay together.

Grandma reflects on her own childhood after her mother died. When she and her siblings were sent off to live with different relatives, it was one of the toughest times in her life. She does not want her grandchildren separated.

"I'll take them in," Grandma tells the CFSA social worker.

Grandma and Grandpa both have jobs but do not make a lot of money. They cover their bills without much leftover. They already have Vernon and Veronica staying with them at their home. But Grandma strongly believes taking in Vontae, Michael, and Ebony is the right thing to do.

Grandma's Rule
"When faced with a challenge," Grandma says, "trust in God."

She spends the next several weeks and months heading to the courts to sort everything out. Vontae, Michael, and Ebony can all stay together, but their lives will still not be easy.

Chapter 17

Princess Shares

Grandma and Grandpa are kind and loving, but they are also strict. This means that they have rules and consequences. They often talk about respect: for God, Grandma and Grandpa, their home, other adults, and each other.

With more kids and not enough bedrooms, Grandma and Grandpa buy two sets of bunk beds. Michael and Vontae share a tiny bedroom near the kitchen, while Vernon and Veronica share one upstairs.

Vontae immediately loves living with Grandma and Grandpa. First, he only has to take care of himself now! Grandma changes Ebony's diapers and Grandpa usually feeds her a bottle. Grandma prepares snacks and meals, makes sure they brush their teeth, and tucks them into bed every night.

Vontae also really likes the new neighborhood. There are more kids around, and the streets do not seem so scary. In the house, Vontae likes to fire up the Nintendo 64, a popular video game console. Grandma does not like him to play for too long, but sometimes Grandpa lets him play a little longer.

His favorite game is Super Mario, where a plumber with a mustache, blue overalls, and a red cap must navigate many challenges to save Princess Peach from the scary villain, Bowser.

PRINCESS SHARES

After moving in with Grandma and Grandpa, Vontae figures he will get to see his big brother Vernon more. But Vernon is a teenager, and he always seems to be out. Vernon is only at the house to sleep and sometimes eat.

While Vontae feels comfortable, one person in the house does not love the new arrangement. Veronica (Princess) feels threatened by so many new kids in the house. There are toys everywhere, and they are all hers—and she does not want to share!

Ebony notices a big dollhouse, and girl dolls with fancy outfits on. She picks one up and starts to pretend the doll is walking.

Princess storms into the room and snatches the doll out of Ebony's hand. "Leave *my* Barbie alone!" Princess screams, emphasizing the word *my*. "Don't touch her. She's not yours!"

Ebony bursts into tears.

Princess wedges herself between the Barbie dollhouse and Ebony. Grandma hears the fuss and walks into the room.

"What's all this noise about?"

Michael, who witnesses the interaction, explains what

happened. Princess, her face crinkled up, does not refute any of it.

"Those are *my* dolls," Princess says, as tears start to well up in her eyes. "I don't want anyone else to touch them or even look at them!"

Grandma stays calm. She knows all these changes are hard on everyone, including Princess. With Vernon not around much, Princess is used to getting all the attention and playing with any toy whenever she wanted.

But she also will not allow anyone in the house to be selfish. Grandma scans her right index finger across the dresser, where there are two different Barbies and four other friends.

Grandma's Rule

"You've got all those dolls," Grandma says. "You can't play with them all at the same time. You must learn to share."

Grandma speaks gently but firmly. Deep down, Princess knows Grandma is right. It will not be easy, but Princess knows she must accept some changes.

"I guess she can play with them sometimes," Princess says reluctantly.

Grandma nods approvingly. Ebony, who has stopped crying, smiles.

Sharing is not a problem for Vontae. Taking care of Ebony and Michael has made him pretty unselfish.

Chapter 18

Sunday Rules

The kids have some freedom to make choices on Saturdays. But Sundays follow a script.

Grandma wakes the children up at 8 a.m.

If they stay up too late on Saturday, it doesn't matter to Grandma. If they want to snooze a little longer, that doesn't matter either. Twice, when Vontae takes too long to get out of bed, Grandma pours a small glass of cold water over his head.

Vontae quickly learns to hop out of bed as soon as he hears Grandma climbing up the stairs toward his bedroom.

Some mornings, the delicious, salty smell of bacon from the kitchen welcomes them as they rise. Other breakfast options include cereal or homemade oatmeal. Then everyone goes upstairs to get dressed up. The family cannot afford fancy brands and multiple outfits. But each Sunday, the boys' shirts and pants are ironed, their shoes polished, and their hair brushed. The girls' dresses are spotless, and their hair never looks better any other day of the week.

A gray church van picks them up around 9:30.

"OK, the van is here!" Grandpa yells.

Grandma always checks each child before they walk out the front door.

The ride to Newborn Pentecostal Church in Northeast D.C. takes about 20 minutes. During that time, Grandpa asks each child to share one thing that they are thankful for.

"I'm thankful Grandma didn't pour cold water on me this morning!" Vontae says jokingly.

Everyone chuckles, including Grandma.

Newborn Pentecostal Church is small, with fewer than 100 members. Everyone knows everyone, many for decades. Deacon Smith is fond of Grandma and Grandpa, and he knows the back story of their grandchildren. Knowing their finances are tight, Deacon Smith gives each of the boys a $5 bill each month.

"Just a little something so you can get a haircut and a treat," he says in a hushed voice.

Overcome with excitement, Vontae also gets nervous holding onto cash.

During the service, the children know they must be quiet and polite, but sometimes Grandma has to give them "The Look" to straighten them up. Even if you didn't make eye contact with Grandma, you could *feel* her looking at you, which was enough to make you behave.

The church is not large enough to have Sunday School for the children, so Grandma tells her kids to pay attention to the preacher's message, which is called a sermon.

"If you've got a problem," she says, "listen closely to the preacher, and you may hear an answer."

They usually attend both services—one at 9 a.m., the other at 11:30 a.m.—and then catch a ride back home in the church van. They have a small lunch (often peanut butter and jelly with chips) and free time before dinner.

One Sunday evening, Michael makes a big announcement.

"I'm not going to church anymore," he says.

Vontae, Princess, and Ebony look at him with their eyes wide open.

"What did you say?" Vontae asks.

"You heard me," Michael says. "I'm not going to church anymore."

Princess runs into the living room and reports Michael's comment to Grandma, who is making the final touches to their dinner.

"Grandma," Princess excitedly says, "Michael isn't going to church anymore!"

The kids expect Grandma to unleash a wrath of fury on Michael. But she surprises them.

"Well, that's Michael's right," Grandma says, as she transports food from the kitchen to the dining room. "But in this house, everything belongs to Jesus. Yall come eat dinner now."

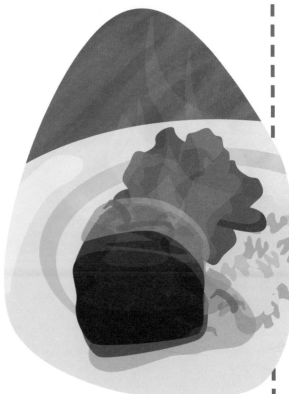

All the kids rush over to the table and see one of their favorite spreads: Salisbury steak, homemade gravy, rice, and broccoli. Money is scarce for Grandma and Grandpa, but they do make sure there's always enough food for the family.

Grandma's Rule

"Always remember that everything comes from God," Grandma says.

Vontae nods, as he scoots toward his chair and starts to plot out how he will work around his plate.

As Michael pulls his chair out, Grandma intercepts him.

"Oh no, Michael," she says. "This is Jesus' food."

Stubbornly, Michael storms away from the table and heads toward the basement.

As for me and my house, we will Serve the Lord

"I don't want nothing to eat anyway," he says.

With Michael downstairs, the dinner conversation is not as lively as usual. Vontae feels bad that Michael cannot eat one of his favorite meals. He assumes Michael will change his mind and join them. But he finishes his first plate and then his second... and still no Michael.

The kids clear the table, and Grandma and Grandpa wash and dry the utensils, plates, and bowls by 6:30 p.m. They all sit in the living room to watch some television.

By 8 p.m., Michael is still in the basement by himself. But at 9 p.m., just as the kids are about to head upstairs to brush their teeth and lay down, Michael slinks into the living room.

"Ma, can I have some Jesus food," he says.

"You sure can," Grandma eagerly says.

She gets up from her chair, heads to the kitchen, and prepares a heaping plate of food for Michael.

Chapter 19

Vontae Raids the Fridge

Grandma and Grandpa did not plan to raise more kids, especially five of them! They must make hard decisions on how to spend their money, so they explain to the children the difference between wants and needs.

"Vernon, do you *need* the latest Michael Jordan sneakers?" Grandpa Lynwood asks.

Vernon wonders if this is a trick question.

"No," he reluctantly says, "but I sure want them!"

"Ebony, do you need to eat dinner tonight?" Grandpa asks.

Ebony vigorously nods.

"That's right," Grandpa says.

The kids do not have an abundance of choices when it comes to toys and clothes. In fact, they each do their best to stretch two pairs of shoes an entire year—as long as their feet don't grow too much.

Grandma and Grandpa prioritize food for the family and even neighbors and friends. Though they don't have much, they always oblige if someone asks for food. Besides, Grandma works magic in the kitchen.

The kids always have three meals a day, and snacks like brownies, cakes, and honey buns. But Grandma notices a problem. She carefully plans out everything the family can eat during a week, but she keeps running short, which means she is spending more money than she budgets for.

Grandma knows she's got growing kids, including a teenager in Vernon. But something just does not add up. So, she investigates.

Though he's not particularly big, Vontae has a large appetite. After school, he eats three to four peanut butter sandwiches. At dinner, he always asks for seconds, and then he eats a snack right before bedtime.

One Saturday morning, when Grandma opens the fridge, she realizes something: the leftover honey barbecue chicken she'd planned to serve for dinner that night is gone! For the rest of the day, she keeps an eye on the kitchen, watching who goes in, and what food comes out. She does not see anything unusual.

After the kids go to bed, Grandma stays up later than normal and listens for any movement in the house. At 1:24 a.m., she hears some noise downstairs. She quietly walks toward the kitchen, hoping not to startle anyone. She suspects she will discover the culprit responsible for the disappearance of food in their house.

As she tiptoes down the final few steps and turns into the kitchen, Grandma sees young Vontae standing up and eating a big bowl of cereal.

"What are you doing, Vontae?" Grandma asks.

"Sorry, Grandma," Vontae says. "I get hungry."

Grandma shakes her head.

"Hurry up and finish that food and get back to bed," Grandma sternly says.

The next night, well after midnight, Vontae wakes up hungry again, and he heads downstairs to the kitchen. But when he pulls the handle, the refrigerator does not open.

Still groggy, Vontae blinks a few times then looks at the fridge. There's a lock, so the freezer and fridge do not open. He cannot get anything out of the fridge. Vontae frowns. But he is more tired than hungry, so he slowly walks back to his room, lays in his bed, and immediately falls back asleep.

In the morning, Grandma wants to speak to Vontae.

"Tae, you cannot sneak food late at night," Grandma says. "For one, we plan out the meals and someone eating a lot more than their share is not fair. And second, we just cannot afford to buy a bunch of extra food. Money is tight as it is. Understand?"

Vontae nods. Then he responds in a new way to his Grandma.

"Yes, Momma," he says.

Grandma nods and smiles. Vontae smiles back at her. It all feels natural to him.

Chapter 20

Cleaning with Grandma

Grandma and Grandpa live in a modest neighborhood in D.C., where families walk and ride the bus. They don't cruise around in expensive, foreign cars. Grandma mostly works Monday through Friday, but she sometimes works on Saturdays.

She cleans houses for a living, and wealthy families sometimes prefer she cleans up while they are out of town or away for the day. That way, when they return, their house is nice and tidy.

If Vernon and Grandpa are busy, Grandma takes the other kids with her while she works. The others do not like to tag along, but Vontae does. He enjoys the drive to nice neighborhoods, where there are gorgeous lawns, perfect fences, and houses with large, inviting windows. In their neighborhood, some windows have bars on them, and most of the windows have the curtains closed tight.

One house Vontae always wants to see is on Rittenhouse Street. When you pull up toward the driveway, big, old trees welcome visitors, and there's a white picket fence. There's a flower garden with white and purple flowers, and a big porch with lots of furniture. The backyard has plush, green grass with assorted balls and toys laying around. On the back deck is more furniture near a large grill with a stovetop attached.

But the nicest furniture is inside the house. That furniture is so nice Vontae is afraid to sit on the couches because the white is very bright.

In the dining room is a big, wooden table with eight large chairs. Above the table is something Grandma calls a *chandelier*. She explains that a chandelier is a fancy light that hangs from the ceiling. Near the front door is a wide, wooden staircase that heads to the top level, where there are four large bedrooms. Vontae fantasizes about what that would be like: to have his very own room.

His favorite part of the house is the kitchen. The wooden cabinets are tall and deep, and the fridge looks just like the cabinets. He is not allowed to eat any of the food, but he does sneak a peek and wishes he could drink a Coke or eat a slice of chocolate cake.

The owners of the home gives Grandma permission to bring the kids and allow them to watch their television. Vontae falls in love; the screen is huge and clear.

While the other kids sit in front of the TV, Vontae likes to watch his Grandma work and occasionally offers to help her. She is a constant blur, methodically cleaning one room at a time. She quietly sings church hymns as she scrubs, scrapes, sweeps, vacuums, and mops the massive home. She only takes a quick break to check on the kids once or twice an hour.

Vontae admires her focus and the pride she puts into a job.

Grandma's Rule

"Whatever you do for work," she says, "do it well, and do it proudly."

Unlike some jobs where people often start at 9 a.m. and end by 5 p.m., Grandma does not work specific hours. She works until the five-bedroom, three-bathroom house on Rittenhouse is clean. Sometimes it takes her five hours, sometimes it takes her eight hours.

Grandma does the work, until the home is clean to her satisfaction. She must do a good job; the family has paid her to clean their home for 10 years, and they give her a generous bonus just before Christmas.

Vontae wonders what it would be like to own a home like this, with all the rooms and cool features. He doesn't know anyone who lives in such a grand house, and he feels crazy for even thinking that big. He doesn't even have his own bedroom, and he wears hand-me-down clothes from his big brother. Still, in the days and weeks after, Vontae pictures the Rittenhouse Street home in his head.

A boy can dream.

Chapter 21

Mr. Robinson Sees Potential

Vontae has always had female teachers at school. He does not know what to make of Mr. Robinson, his first male teacher. Vontae decides he needs to figure out what he can get away with in Mr. Robinson's class.

Early in fifth grade, he cracks jokes and makes faces. He picks verbal fights with classmates. He storms out of class without permission. Through it all, Mr. Robinson remains cool and speaks with a calm voice.

"I've got to see how far I can push him," Vontae whispers to his classmate Devin. "Something has to set him off!"

Vontae's persistence to misbehave and to defy Mr. Robinson does not change the outcome. Mr. Robinson maintains his composure, and he usually pulls Vontae out of the classroom, highlights his misdeed and punishment, and lets him settle down.

Mr. Robinson's patience comes from his own experience. As a boy, his mother instilled in him a passion for education, and she ascended to become one of the first African American principals in D.C. Still, Charles Robinson and his mother often had to battle for his inclusion in gifted and talented classes at the Christian schools he attended.

That is why Mr. Robinson commits himself to educating and empowering African American students, particularly boys, who are often overlooked and excluded from the best educational opportunities in D.C.

Mr. Robinson is especially sensitive about Vontae because he knows his story; Mr. Robinson taught Vernon as well. Vontae likes to read, but he does not like to write. Mr. Robinson pushes him to do more papers, but Vontae resists or refuses.

Soon Vontae realizes Mr. Robinson has the ultimate motivational tool—he coaches the basketball and flag football teams. Vontae grabs the pen dangling on Mr. Robinson's door to write his name on the flag football signup sheet, but someone stops him before any ink comes out.

"No, sir," Mr. Robinson says softly to Vontae. "You cannot play flag football."

Vontae looks puzzled.

"Why not?" he asks.

Mr. Robinson takes the pen from Vontae's hand and presses it into the cap connected to the door.

Mr. Robinson's Rule

"You have to excel in school in order to play sports. No grades, no games," he says.

Mr. Robinson explains that playing school sports is a privilege at Truesdell Elementary, not a right. He makes all the decisions for the flag football and basketball teams.

Vontae takes a deep breath. On the one hand, he does not like that Mr. Robinson has so much power. But on the other hand, Vontae really, really wants to play both of those sports. He decides to try harder with his classwork and homework. Two days later, just before the flag football team's first practice, Vontae hands in a math assignment on decimals.

Mr. Robinson reviews the students' homework while they work on a group project. He marks up each assignment with lots of red ink; they're struggling to multiply decimals, failing to properly carry the decimal point to the correct position. But he notices something about Vontae's work: he got all the problems correct! Even more impressive is that Vontae shows his work, and it checks out.

When the bell rings and the students file out of class, Mr. Robinson asks Vontae to stay behind and have a chat with him.

Vontae gulps because he is nervous.

"Vontae, you did an excellent job on your math homework," Mr. Robinson says. "You have a great understanding of it. Would you consider working with me to help some of your classmates tomorrow?"

Vontae nods.

"Is that it?" he asks.

Mr. Robinson moves from sitting in his chair to sitting on the corner of his desk.

"If you keep working hard in class," Mr. Robinson says, "you can join the flag football team."

Vontae lights up.

Over time, Vontae comes to admire Mr. Robinson. He likes that Mr. Robinson is always available, before school starts and long after school ends. Just as he does in the classroom, Mr. Robinson never yells or screams when he is coaching.

The flag football team dominates the regular season, with Vontae's speed helping the team as a running back and even more as a safety. They win every regular-season game and reach the city championship game against Brown Elementary.

The game is supposed to be played at a neutral field, which means not at Truesdell or Brown. But the championship game is set at Brown Elementary. Mr. Robinson's team arrives just minutes before kickoff because their bus gets stuck in traffic due to a four-car accident. His players are rattled and nervous, especially with over 100 fans packed in the stands to support Brown. Vontae plays without fear, and he scores his team's only touchdown.

For the first time in the season, Truesdell's defense gives up points, and Brown wins the game 13–6.

Later in the school year, Vontae plays his favorite sport: basketball. With his quickness, he gives opponents fits, and he helps Truesdell finish with a winning record. As the school year winds down, Mr. Robinson asks Vontae to stay after class one Wednesday afternoon.

"Vontae," Mr. Robinson says, "you have so much potential. I know you love sports, and you should stick with them. But keep up with your school work because you're very bright."

Vontae swells with pride. Everyone always tells Vernon he'll be an NFL star. But Vontae? Grandma and Aunt Missy each tell him that he's going to be successful someday. Mr. Robinson is the first person outside of the family to hype him up.

REPORT CARD

A+	MATH
B	SCIENCE
B+	SOCIAL STUDIES
A	GYM
A-	ART

Vontae does not know what to say after all of Mr. Robinson's kind comments. So, he just nods.

Five weeks later, Grandma and Grandpa are at school for his fifth-grade graduation. Vontae is on the cusp of middle school! After a short ceremony, Grandma rushes to Mr. Robinson.

"Thank you, Mr. Robinson," Grandma says. "You've done so much for our Vontae!"

About 15 yards away, Vontae sees Grandma and Mr. Robinson, and he makes a beeline toward them. As he approaches Mr. Robinson, Vontae wraps his arms around his teacher and hugs him. He does not say anything, but Vontae hugs Mr. Robinson for several seconds.

Mr. Robinson also does not speak. The two just revel in the moment.

Chapter 22

Vontae Tells the Truth

For the most part, Vontae excels in school, keeping up with his work and obeying his teachers. But there is always a common link to when he makes poor choices: Carl.

Carl likes to make people laugh and test his teachers' patience. Though that's not his inclination, Vontae sometimes goes along with Carl's ideas. They combine to create enough distractions and problems in fifth grade that their teacher, Mrs. Gentry, separates them for sixth grade.

"I don't think Carl is a good influence on your grandson," Mrs. Gentry tells Grandma at the end of the school year. "Maybe keep Vontae away from him."

The boys' friendship remains intact. Vontae does not have many friends, and he likes that he has a lot in common with Carl: basketball, other sports, and video games.

During lunch one day in sixth grade, Vontae distracts Mr. Peabody by asking him questions about his weekend plans. Then Carl stealthily walks behind them, grabs his covered coffee mug and walks to the water fountain. Carl quickly dumps out the coffee and fills the mug with water. He returns the mug to the podium Mr. Peabody is standing by. Then Vontae abruptly ends his conversation with the teacher and walks away.

From across the lunch room, Vontae and Carl watch Mr. Peabody reach for his mug and take a sip. He crinkles up his face.

Surprises sweeps over him as he tastes cold water and not warm coffee with cream.

The boys burst out laughing.

After school on a Friday, Carl asks Vontae if he wants to spend the night at his house.

"I've got this new wrestling game that just came out!" Carl tells Vontae. "I need someone to play it with, and my mom bought me a bunch of snacks."

This sounds wonderful to Vontae. But he knows his Grandma and Grandpa do not like him staying at other people's homes. He comes up with a plan. He rushes into the house and finds Grandma.

"Grandma, Grandma!" Vontae excitedly says. "Can I spend the night at Aunt Missy's house?"

Grandma turns her head sideways and furrows her brow. "Why?"

Vontae, who anticipates that question, quickly answers.

"I just haven't seen her in a really long time," Vontae says.

Grandma seems suspicious but gives him permission. He runs to his room, gathers a change of clothes, and stuffs them into a backpack.

"Don't forget your toothbrush!" Grandma yells from her bedroom.

Vontae sprints to the bathroom, grabs his toothbrush, and bolts downstairs.

"I got it Grandma!" he says, blowing out the front door.

Grandma does not even have time to ask him how he will get to Aunt Missy's; she does not live within walking distance. But she wants to get a jumpstart on dinner and figures Vontae had made some kind of arrangement.

Vontae almost skips to Carl's house—his plan worked!

It's everything they hoped for: playing the wrestling game for hours, eating snacks—Doritos and Oodles of Noodles—whenever they feel the slightest bit hungry. But around 8 p.m., Vontae feels something sweep over him. His smile disappears.

"I need to use your phone," Vontae tells Carl. He doesn't even finish the match he and Carl are playing.

A look of confusion crosses Carl's face.

Vontae picks up the telephone in the kitchen and dials the number.

"Hi Momma," Vontae says. "I can't lie to you. I wasn't going to spend the night at Aunt Missy's. I'm at Carl's, but I'm coming home. Please open the door for me."

When he returns home, Vontae walks in with his head low, and looks up at his grandma. Tears start to build in his eyes because he knows he has disappointed her.

Grandma's Rule

"A lie will lead to trouble. Then when you tell the truth, nobody will believe you. A liar will not enter the gates of heaven," Grandma says.

Then her serious face turns sweet.

"No video games for a week," she says softly. "But I am proud of you for doing the right thing."

Grandma opens her arms and invites Vontae in for a hug. He feels relieved as he rests in the comfort of his grandma's love.

Chapter 23

Vontae Returns Money

Middle school does not represent big changes for Vontae. He feels comfortable at Paul Middle School, and he settles in with his teachers and friends.

Vontae appreciates that the most chaotic time of the school day does not affect him. At 2:50 p.m., when the final bell rings, the madness ensues. There are hundreds of elementary and middle school students, and they all seem to be going different places!

Over a dozen buses pack the tight, one-way drive way and efficiently flow past the front of the school and into the city streets.

Vontae and Carl each walk to school; Vontae can usually make a one-way trip in 10 minutes if he walks quickly. They like to hang out after school, and they are glad they do not have to be in a rush.

During the second week of sixth grade, Vontae closes his locker and starts to walk toward the main entrance to meet Carl. A fourth-grade girl, who is in a rush to catch her bus, drops $10 as she hurriedly packs her bag. The bill slowly flutters through the air, and the girl is out the front door before the bill even touches the ground. Amid the chaos, no one sees the money, except Vontae.

He calmly walks over to the spot near the locker where the $10 bill lays on the side with a portrait of President Alexander Hamilton. Vontae looks around, scoops the bill up, and sticks it in the front left pocket of his jeans. His mind races as he thinks about the snacks and treats he can buy with the money!

He excitedly walks outside, then runs toward Carl.

"Guess what?" Vontae says. "This girl dropped $10, and I got it in my pocket!"

Carl smiles, and they start to walk toward a corner store two blocks from school. When they get there, the boys go on a snacking spree: a Mountain Dew for Vontae, a Fanta orange for Carl, a big bag of Cool Ranch Doritos, and Fun Dip, a sugary stick that you dip into a sweet flavored powder.

The boys chow on the snacks at a table in a nearby playground. After crunching two Doritos, Carl pauses and asks his friend a question.

"Vontae, do you feel bad about using the money?"

Vontae takes a break from enjoying his Fun Dip and ponders Carl's question. He does not answer, but he cannot shake the feeling inside him for the rest of the afternoon. The boys play some basketball and a few video games before Vontae heads home for dinner.

Just before dinner, Vontae approaches his Grandpa.

"Grandpa, can I have $10?" he asks.

Grandpa often gets requests for money, and his response is always the same.

"What for?" he says.

Vontae tells his Grandpa about the girl, the money, and the corner store trip.

"Grandpa, I should not have spent that money," Vontae admits.

"I should have kept it and returned it to her tomorrow."

Grandpa smiles.

"Vontae, that is the right thing to do," he says. "I'm proud of you for seeing that you could have handled this better."

Grandpa reaches into his back pocket, pulls out his wallet, and hands Vontae a $10 bill.

The next morning, Vontae walks to school extra early. He waits near the locker where he found the money the day before. He does not know the girl's name, but he recognizes her right away.

"Excuse me," Vontae quietly says. "My name is Vontae, and I'm a sixth-grader here. When you were leaving yesterday, I saw you drop $10, but you left before I could return it to you."

Vontae then reaches in his pocket, pulls out the $10 bill, and hands it to her.

The girl's mouth opens wide.

"That was my lunch money for the whole week," she replies. "I had no idea where it went!"

She then introduces herself.

"My name is Vanessa. Thank you so, so much," she says.

Vontae shakes her hand and smiles back. He thinks about the previous day, when he dug into some of his favorite snacks—he did not enjoy them the way he normally did. As he talks to Vanessa, Vontae feels something more powerful than hunger: relief and pride for doing the right thing.

Chapter 24

Tragic End

Vontae likes his routine. After school, he can walk 12 blocks to Grandma and Grandpa's rowhouse on Emerson Street. But one day instead, Vontae and Carl walk three-and-a-half blocks to the Emery Heights Community Center playground.

Lots of kids from the surrounding neighborhoods (16th Street Heights, Brightwood, Brightwood Park, and Manor Park) play hoops there. Vontae and Carl love the games; they're competitive and fast-paced. The games are proof that there are a lot of good, young basketball players in D.C.

One downside is that some teenagers, and even some young adults, hang around the court, flashing their fancy clothes, shoes, and wads of cash. They are gang members: each gang distinguished by the color they wear.

The gangs are constantly trying to bring in new, members. Public basketball courts and playgrounds around the city have lots of potential recruits.

Vontae is not impressed by the gang members and their things. He is always polite, but he tries to avoid them. He just wants to play basketball.

One of the top regulars at the Emery Heights court goes by the nickname "B." He's three years older than Vontae. B is above average height for his age, and he can jump really, really high. He first dunked a basketball when he was in seventh grade.

Vontae enjoys playing basketball, but he does not mind watching it, especially if B is playing. On a few occasions, when there are not enough big kids, Vontae even gets to play on B's team! That makes Vontae nervous, but he just tries to play good defense, make his layups, and pass the ball to B.

Vontae will never forget the time B complimented him after they skunked an opponent. They beat the other team 15-0!

"Nice game, Little Vernon," B says coolly.

Vontae does not know B's real name, and B apparently doesn't know Vontae's name either.

Carl, Vontae, and about a half-dozen other students from

Paul Junior High School regularly play at the Emery Heights court. A month into the school year, Paul Junior High students notice a familiar face showing up to the court.

His name is Mr. Dunham, and he is the middle school teacher for P.E. Like Mr. Robinson, Mr. Dunham encourages Vontae in the classroom and in sports. But unlike Mr. Robinson, Mr. Dunham is loud—both with his voice and his choice of clothes. He favors clothes that match the color of highlighters. Students can see or hear him coming from quite a distance, between his booming voice and eye-opening outfits.

"How y'all doing?" Mr. Dunham says, as he arrives at the court. "Everyone staying out of trouble?"

Mr. Dunham stops by the court at least three days a week, and he sticks around for 30 to 45 minutes. He was born and raised in Brightwood Park and is the son of a famous local figure. Almost every African American male in the area wants Mr. Dunham's dad to give them a fade: a haircut style. Mr. Dunham's dad is a master with his electric clippers; he can blend a person's hair to very specific lengths and shapes.

Mr. Dunham knows everyone, including the gang members.

"Vontae, you staying out of trouble?" Mr. Dunham asks him one afternoon. "You let me know if anyone out here is bothering you."

Mr. Dunham is much older than anyone else who shows up at the court. But he can still play basketball. When the games wind down as the sun sets, Vontae tries to squeeze in a one-on-one game with Mr. Dunham.

Vontae doesn't get the sense that Mr. Dunham is trying his hardest. But he does challenge Vontae and push him to work on his weaknesses, especially dribbling with his left (non-dominant) hand. Because of his quickness, Vontae can usually figure out a way to get off a right-handed shot. Mr. Dunham, though, always overplays Vontae's right hand and forces him to go left.

"No, no!" Mr. Dunham says, when Vontae attempts a crossover dribble from his left to right hand. "That won't work on me."

Vontae thinks Mr. Dunham is skilled enough to beat B and Vernon!

Vontae gets to play for Mr. Dunham, who coaches the middle-school basketball team at Paul Junior High and also coaches a local spring and summer squad. The kids love to play for him because he is so positive and passionate. Many of the boys don't have extra money, but Mr. Dunham always comes up with enough to buy them snacks and meals.

After a strong winter season at school, Vontae is eager to get back outside and play at the Emery Heights court. On the first nice day of spring, Vontae and Carl rush over to the court after school. They want to make sure they get into the first game!

As they near the court, Vontae sees the flashing lights atop several police cars. There's a crowd of people across the street from the community garden.

"What's going on?" Vontae asks no one in particular, as he tries to peek at what everyone is looking at.

When he finally works his way through the crowd, Vontae immediately recognizes the person lying on the ground. B is on his side, and he is not moving.

The policemen are moving quickly, some taking pictures, others speaking on radios, and others trying to keep people behind the yellow tape.

"Is B OK?" Vontae asks Charles, an older boy and a regular at the Emery Heights court.

"Nah, man," Charles says. "They say he got shot a bunch of times. He just joined a gang."

Vontae looks at B again, and he notices that B is wearing the royal blue associated with one of the local gangs. Tears well up in Vontae's eyes. His heart aches. From out of nowhere, Vontae feels a hand clutch his left shoulder. When he turns, Vontae sees his big brother. Vernon wraps his arms around Vontae and hugs him.

"Let's go home, little bro," Vernon says quietly.

Vontae struggles because he admired his brother's friend. B had been nice to him, and he was such a great athlete. Why did the gang battles have to take someone with so much promise?

Chapter 25

Miss Giles and Detention

Paul Junior High serves hundreds of students. There's someone every student knows but does not want to know too well.

Her name is Miss Giles.

Most students cannot tell you what her title is at Paul Junior High, only that she has an office and that she hands out the discipline. An African American woman with short hair, Miss Giles is tough and serious, an intimidating presence despite her petite size. When she walks down the hall, a lot of students avoid making eye contact with her.

Students fear Miss Giles: she makes more students cry than anyone else at Paul Junior High!

If students break a rule or behave poorly, they receive a yellow write-up slip from the teacher. Then Miss Giles determines whether the student pays the price in Room 110 or Room 210: short-term detention or long-term detention.

Carl is a fixture in 210 because he often comes to school late, skips class, or gets in trouble for acting up. Still, Carl does not like 210 because Mr. Price is very strict.

"He's like a drill sergeant," Carl says to Vontae. "He makes it feel like jail in school!"

Students in 210 line up on the wall at the start and end of class. They do not play games, they must remain quiet, and they must ask permission even to stand up and stretch. Even worse, the students in 210 are the absolute last people in the entire school to eat lunch. Everything is cold and the best snacks have run out.

The 110 teacher, Mrs. Long, is kinder and more reasonable. She even cracks a joke once in a while.

Vontae avoids a visit to Miss Giles' office until the end of sixth grade.

In Mrs. Jackson's class, each student is assigned to make a food representative of his or her culture and bring that dish to share with classmates. A Mexican classmate brings in a flan, a rich, creamy, sweet dessert. A classmate whose mother is from Norway brings in Lefse, a soft flatbread made of potatoes, flour, butter, and cream. A classmate whose father is from Jamaica brings in jerk chicken, which is chicken with a spicy mixture rubbed onto the meat.

The students cannot resist laughing at the dish's name!

Vontae helps Grandma make her famous honey buns. They are a hit with his classmates too. As they near the end of class, Vontae gets anxious. The small bites of the different dishes make him hungry for lunch. His impatience grows.

Gerald takes out a loaf pan from a double-sacked grocery bag. The top is covered in aluminum foil. Vontae does not like the smell.

"This is my mom's famous meatloaf," he proudly says. "I'm sure you've had meatloaf before, but my mom makes the best! Hers is also healthier because my little sister cannot eat beef, so my mom makes this with ground turkey instead."

Gerald takes out a spatula and starts to dish out bite-sized pieces on small blue paper plates. Mrs. Jackson's rule is that everyone must try every dish unless they are allergic.

Vontae does not want to try the meatloaf. For one, it is a cold blob. Meatloaf should be hot! Second, the meatloaf does not look tasty. Other students also do not seem excited to try the meatloaf. Vontae, mindful of Mrs. Jackson's rule, takes a spoon and scoops up the meatloaf.

"Yuck!" he says. "This is nasty!"

Other classmates immediately start to laugh; Gerald bursts into tears. Mrs. Jackson frowns and scolds Vontae.

"Vontae!" she sternly says. "See me after class."

Vontae stops laughing. Now he is afraid. *Will he be sent to see Miss Giles?*

When class ends, Mrs. Jackson sits at her desk and fills out a yellow slip.

"You know why you're receiving this," Mrs. Jackson says to Vontae. Then she says the four words Paul Junior High students dread.

"Go see Miss Giles."

The walk feels long, as many things run through Vontae's mind. *Will Miss Giles send me to 110 or 210? What will Grandma say? How long will Grandma punish me?*

The wait is also long. When Vontae arrives, two other students are waiting to see Miss Giles with yellow slips.

When it's finally his turn, Vontae slowly enters Miss Giles' office. Unlike other people's offices, Miss Giles does not have any family or vacation pictures. Her desk is clean, her walls empty—except for one simple poster with a Bible verse: Proverbs 10:17.

"Whoever heeds discipline shows the way to life, but whoever ignores correction leads others astray."

Vontae takes it all in.

"Take a seat," she says firmly as she takes the yellow slip and starts to read.

"What should we do with you?" Miss Giles says.

Vontae does not know whether she is really asking him a question. He hesitates for a moment.

"I don't know, Miss Giles," he says nervously. "Maybe just give me a warning?"

Miss Giles shakes her head.

"I was not looking for an answer," she says.

Miss Giles' Rule
"You have no say in the consequences based on your bad decision."

Miss Giles fills out a sheet of paper that has *Discipline Report* in big, bold letters at the top.

"You need to get this signed tonight and bring it back in the morning," Miss Giles says. "I have a slot in my door you can drop it in."

Vontae is still unsure of one other key detail. He is afraid to ask though.

"Collect all your books and go see Mrs. Long in Room 110," Miss Giles says. "You'll be spending the rest of the week there."

Vontae takes a deep breath. He will not see his friend Carl, but he also will not have to spend time with mean Mr. Price!

After school, Vontae does something unexpected. He takes the bus from school and heads to his mom's apartment. He knocks on her front door. His mom never answers right away. He waits a few more seconds, then he knocks again.

"Who is it?" Mom asks, with annoyance in her voice.

"It's me, Mom," Vontae says.

Mom opens the door and hugs Vontae.

"How are you doing?" she asks, as she holds him for a few extra moments.

Vontae fills her in on basketball, middle school, and his siblings. She makes him nachos and pours him some root beer. Vontae is glad to see his mom; he has not talked to her for a few weeks. But he does not share the real reason he is there.

"Mom, before I leave, can you sign this?" Vontae asks.

He hands her the Discipline Report from Miss Giles.

"No big deal," he says. "A little misunderstanding in class. Just need your signature."

Mom makes a face but signs the paper anyway.

Vontae hugs his mom, heads out the door, and walks toward the bus stop.

The next afternoon, while in 110, Vontae is called to Miss Long's desk.

"Miss Giles needs to see you," Miss Long says to Vontae.

Vontae is confused. He is not sure why he has to go back and see her again. This is not how it is supposed to work. Vontae walks to her office. There is no line, so he knocks on the door.

"Come in," Miss Giles says.

Vontae enters the office. He sits after Miss Giles invites him to take a seat.

"Do you know why you are here?" Miss Giles asks.

Vontae does not know whether he is supposed to answer. After waiting a moment, Vontae takes a deep breath then speaks.

"No ma'am," he says.

"Whose signature is this?" Miss Giles says, pointing to his Discipline Report.

"It's my mom's," Vontae confidently says.

Miss Giles shakes her head.

"Vontae, I know all about you," she says. "You do not live with your mom. Whose signature should you have gotten on this?"

Vontae knows the answer.

"My Grandma," Vontae says quietly.

Miss Giles nods. She starts to write out a new Discipline Report, with the same information as the one from the previous day.

"Get this signed by your Grandma before tomorrow," Miss Giles says, "or else you can go up to 210 for the rest of the month."

Vontae does not want to mess around. There are still 15 school days in the month, and he knows Miss Giles is serious. He re-reads the poster with the Bible verse.

"Whoever heeds discipline shows the way to life, but whoever ignores correction leads others astray."

Vontae decides he will head home, tell his Grandma everything she needs to know, and then ask for her signature.

Chapter 26

The Impressive Jump

Vontae tries to see all of Vernon's football games at Dunbar High School. He is so proud of his big brother. Many people say Vernon is the most dominant football player ever from D.C.! Vontae figures that must be true because lots of colleges come to Dunbar to meet Vernon. Vontae has heard of two of those schools: the University of Virginia and the University of Maryland. They are close to D.C. He recognizes another one because they are very famous for football.

When the University of Florida comes to see Vernon, Vontae makes sure that he can tag along. Many colleges are recruiting Vernon, which means each is interested in his potential as a football player in their powerful programs. All the colleges are part of the National Collegiate Athletic Association (commonly known by its acronym, NCAA) and participate in Division I football—the highest level after high school and before the National Football League. Each season, NCAA Division I colleges can offer a certain number of athletic scholarships to football players to join their programs. The very best recruits get full rides, which means the school covers all the cost of their education and anything to do with football.

127

Vernon is *that* good. Colleges are offering him a full ride scholarship!

Normally college coaches visit the homes of recruits. But Grandma does not want anyone coming to her house. She prefers to see the coaches at Dunbar. Coach Jeffries always arranges to have Vernon and his family use the teacher's lounge not long after the school day ends.

Ron Zook is the head coach at the University of Florida. Vontae is already impressed because Coach Zook wears a blue polo shirt with a cool looking alligator on it (the school's team name is the Gators). Coach Zook meets the family in the teacher's lounge, but they walk and talk and end up outside in the football stadium.

After 15 minutes, Coach Zook starts to shiver.

"I'm getting cold," he says. "Can we head back inside?"

It is November, and the temperature is 40 degrees Fahrenheit. The group starts to walk back toward a set of doors leading to the lounge.

Coach Jeffries tugs at the thick, double doors. Security is something that Dunbar High takes seriously because they are in the city and they want to protect students and staff. In fact, the school has four metal detectors at two main entrances that everyone must either enter or exit the building from. The metal detectors are similar to the detectors at airports.

The large, windowless doors are not opening for Coach Jeffries, and he knows he does not have the keys to open them.

"Uh-oh," he says. "We're locked out. How are we going to get back into the building?"

No one has a good suggestion.

Without saying a word, Vontae literally springs into action. He jumps high to grasp the top of the large door frame, pulls himself up and looks through a plexiglass window into the building.

"Oh, I see the custodian down the hall!" Vontae says.

He bangs on the plexiglass window and waves the custodian toward the door.

Everyone else is peering up in awe.

"That door frame has to be 9-feet high," Coach Zook says. "He made that look like nothing. How old is he?"

Vernon smiles and answers proudly.

"Coach, he's only 13 years old," he says. "And he's a great student-athlete."

Coach Zook shakes his head and smiles.

"Well, I had intended to just offer you a scholarship, Vernon," Coach Zook says. "But Vontae, I'm thinking about offering you one right now too!"

Vontae does not think what he did is a big deal. After all, he just wants to help his big brother impress the big-shot football coach. He knows Coach Zook is not serious, but the compliment boosts his confidence.

Maybe I can play for him someday, Vontae thinks.

Chapter 27

Trying Something New

Vontae's favorite subject in school is math. He likes solving problems. His least favorite subject is history. He thinks it's boring to read books and look at fuzzy black–and–white photos of faces and places. Then he is assigned to Mr. Ward's eighth–grade history class.

Vontae has never met anyone like him. Mr. Ward doesn't start class immediately when the bell rings. Instead, he lets students take a few minutes to read different magazines and newspapers, including the Washington Post. Mr. Ward also tells them tales of his educational adventures to Russia, Asia, and Africa.

"Traveling the world shaped who I am today," Mr. Ward tells his students. "It empowered me."

Mr. Ward does not like to stand at the front of the classroom and lecture the students. He wants them to *experience* history.

For a Civil War assignment, Mr. Ward has each student study two different battles and put together a PowerPoint presentation. The student then explains, in front of classmates, which side won and why. Vontae learns about the strategies of the generals, including Ulysses S. Grant.

Every Friday, students must also speak in front of the class for at least two minutes on a current event, meaning something happening right now. The student must go through the *Five Ws*: Who, What, When, Where, and Why.

What frustrates many of the students is that Mr. Ward randomly picks two of the 24 students in the class.

"What a waste of time," a classmate mutters to Vontae when they are not selected. "I did all that reading for nothing!"

Vontae shrugs. He does not mind when Mr. Ward does not pick him to discuss a current event. Nor does Vontae mind when Mr. Ward assigns homework every night. In fact, Vontae likes Mr. Ward so much he signs up for a special after-school group. It's called the Young Ambassadors. In this group, Mr. Ward mentors six male students. He wants to inspire and empower them to be scholars. Vontae especially loves that Young Ambassadors do not go to school on a lot of Fridays!

Miss Middleton, the principal, allows Mr. Ward to take his Young Ambassadors on field trips. Sometimes they do not even report to school. Instead, the students meet Mr. Ward at a designated location like the Smithsonian, the world's largest museum, research, and education complex. Other times, they leave school early and eat lunch at different restaurants.

One meal they experience is at a Japanese restaurant. Vontae knows that Japan is an island country in the Pacific Ocean. He also knows that Japan is part of Asia, near China. Vontae thinks Japanese food must be like Chinese food. He loves Chinese food, especially egg rolls, chicken wings, and egg foo young. Egg foo young is like a Chinese omelet with meat and veggies.

Vontae gets nervous as soon as he walks into the restaurant. It is much nicer than the Chinese restaurants Vontae regularly eats at. When he gets the menu, he does not recognize any of the dishes.

"Today we are going to eat sushi," Mr. Ward says. "It is a Japanese delicacy that centers around raw fish."

Vontae scrunches his face and swallows nervously. He does not want to eat raw fish!

"What I like about sushi is how much attention the chefs give each piece," Mr. Ward says. "Some sushi is just the fish. Other sushi is coupled with a perfect portion of rice and different spices and vegetables. Has anyone ever had sushi before?"

None of the six boys raise their hands.

"Does tuna count?" Eric asks. "My mom sometimes serves it out of a can."

Mr. Ward laughs.

"No, not quite," he responds.

Mr. Ward orders for them. Vontae does not recognize anything except the words *tuna* and *salmon*.

While they wait for their food, Mr. Ward picks up a small wooden block.

"These are chopsticks," he says.

He separates the block into two sticks and comfortably handles them in his right hand. He explains to the boys how to grip each chopstick, and guide one between the index and thumb to pick up food.

All the words start to blur together for Vontae. He hears so many new words, such as *wasabi, unagi,* and *nori,* also known as seaweed.

"Seaweed is a staple of the ocean and Japanese cuisine," Mr. Ward says. "It is rich in fiber."

When the food arrives, the different colors stand out. Mr. Ward instructs the boys to pour soy sauce into a half-dollar sized bowl.

"Now dip one chopstick into the bright green paste," Mr. Ward says. "That is wasabi; it is Japanese horseradish. It is very spicy! Take a tiny bit and mix it with the soy sauce. If you feel adventurous, put a little in your mouth."

Eric is the first to try. He dips his chopstick into the green paste and sticks the chopstick in his mouth. Mr. Ward tries to stop him, but it's too late.

"My mouth is on fire," Eric screams. "Hot, hot, hot!"

Eric grabs his glass of water and chugs all of it.

"I was trying to say that you put too much on your chopstick," Mr. Ward says.

Everyone laughs—except Vontae. Vontae does not want to try sushi.

"I'm good, Mr. Ward," he says. "I don't like sushi."

Mr. Ward does not accept Vontae's answer and encourages him to taste it.

Mr. Ward's Rule

"You never know what you like until you try it," he says.

Vontae reconsiders. He is hungry, after all, and he does not want to disappoint Mr. Ward.

"Let's try unagi first," Mr. Ward says, pointing to one plate.

Vontae sees a brownish piece of meat on top of rice. Seaweed wraps around the rice and meat, and there's a drizzle of brown sauce.

Mr. Ward goes to great lengths to explain everything, but he does not explain what unagi is. Vontae gulps. He does not quite know how to use chopsticks, so he picks up the unagi with his fingers and places it in his mouth.

Vontae chews and chews... and he is delighted by the flavors.

"Yum," Vontae says, surprised. "This is really good, Mr. Ward. What is it?"

"It's freshwater eel," Mr. Ward says.

Vontae stops chewing for a moment, but he decides it's too tasty to pass up. With his big appetite, Vontae ends up eating more sushi than anyone else. In all, he eats 14 pieces of sushi.

As the server clears the table, there's no food left on any of the plates. Vontae feels satisfaction—and a full belly.

The only thing left is plenty of wasabi. But no one wants to make the same mistake Eric did!

Vontae is grateful Mr. Ward treats him to new foods and other experiences.

"Thanks, Mr. Ward," Vontae says, "for everything."

Chapter 28

Adaline Teaches Vontae to Be Himself

Vontae prides himself on his athleticism. But his big brother Vernon casts a mighty shadow.

Vernon leads Dunbar to two city championships. He plays tight end, safety, receiver, kick returner, linebacker, and even defensive end. In his senior year, Vernon catches 21 passes for 511 yards and five touchdowns despite missing three games with an injury. In track, he wins the high jump and the 100- and 200-meter titles.

Others constantly remind Vontae of his legendary brother.

All the hype makes Vontae uncomfortable. He loves Vernon and roots for him harder than anyone else. But in lifting Vernon up, Vontae gets knocked down. He does not think people mean to be, well, mean.

"Can you play all those positions like Vernon?" "Can you run and jump like he does?"

Vernon helps establish Dunbar as a football powerhouse. Coupled with its excellent education, Dunbar starts to attract

more talented football players. So, when Vontae arrives on campus as a freshman, the Crimson Tide—Dunbar's nickname—is loaded with upperclassmen. Besides, Vontae's school did not have a football team in seventh or eighth grade.

Coach Jefferies and his staff must teach Vontae all the fundamentals. Initially, the coaches have Vontae learn to play safety on defense. There are two safeties, and they are defensive backs who line up before every play furthest from the ball. Cornerbacks are also defensive backs, but they usually shadow the other team's wide receivers. On each play, safeties have different responsibilities, but mostly they are the last line of defense. To thrive at safety, a player must be athletic and smart.

Vontae fits the bill! The transition is difficult for him, though, and Vontae hardly steps on the field in a game.

In D.C., the Mercy Rule always keeps the clock running on Dunbar. That rule mandates the clock does not stop once a team is up by 35 points. The rule helps accelerate the completion of the game so the score does not get even more one-sided.

Dunbar dominates, so the Mercy Rule is in effect in many of its games. When that happens in the third game, against Parkdale High, Vontae hears his number called.

"Go in at free safety," says Coach Cox, who oversees the defensive backs.

Vontae's eyes get big. He did not think he would be playing. He struggles to find his mouth guard, and he barely gets into position before the ball is snapped by the opposing quarterback. The first play is a run, and Dunbar's defensive linemen quickly stop the play. But on the next play, the quarterback pretends to give the ball to a running back. Vontae takes a step forward, in the direction of the running back. But he notices that the receiver starts to sprint in the other direction.

"It's a play action fake!" Coach Cox screams from the sideline. (This is when the quarterback tries to trick the defense into thinking the offense is going to run the ball but instead they are going to throw it.)

Dunbar's defense bites. More than any defender, the free safety must stay disciplined and not fall for the fake handoff. The ball flies through the air, and Vontae tries to close the gap between himself and the receiver. But the receiver hauls in the pass cleanly and scores a 40-yard touchdown.

Vontae surrenders a touchdown on his second play.

Afterwards, Grandma picks Vontae up outside Dunbar's locker room, where teammates are listening to music and singing and dancing.

"You played in your first high school game!" she says.

Vontae does not feel like celebrating. He cannot imagine a worse way to make his athletic debut at Dunbar High. The ride home is a quiet one.

Vontae breaks the silence.

"Momma, do you love Vernon more because he is a better football player than me?"

Grandma chuckles but realizes Vontae is serious. Her smile quickly disappears from her face.

"Vontae, you know I do not like you boys playing football," she says. "I think the game is too physical; lots of kids get hurt playing that game! But I care for each of you children and never compare. Do you know why?"

Vontae has no clue and shrugs his shoulders.

"I don't know, Momma," he quietly says.

"Because God does not compare any man, woman, or child," she says. "He loves us all the same and gives us all our own journey in this world."

Vontae nods. That makes sense to him.

Grandma's Rule
"Win or lose, I'll still love you the same." Grandma says.

A sense of relief sweeps over Vontae. Sports have always come easy to him, and he feels best after he performs well. When he does not, his confidence sinks.

"I am no football expert," Grandma says. "But I think you

should be patient with yourself and listen to your coaches. They apparently know what they are doing."

Vontae does not speak; he spends the rest of the ride home thinking. When they get to their front door, Vontae hugs his Grandma long and tight.

"Thanks, Momma."

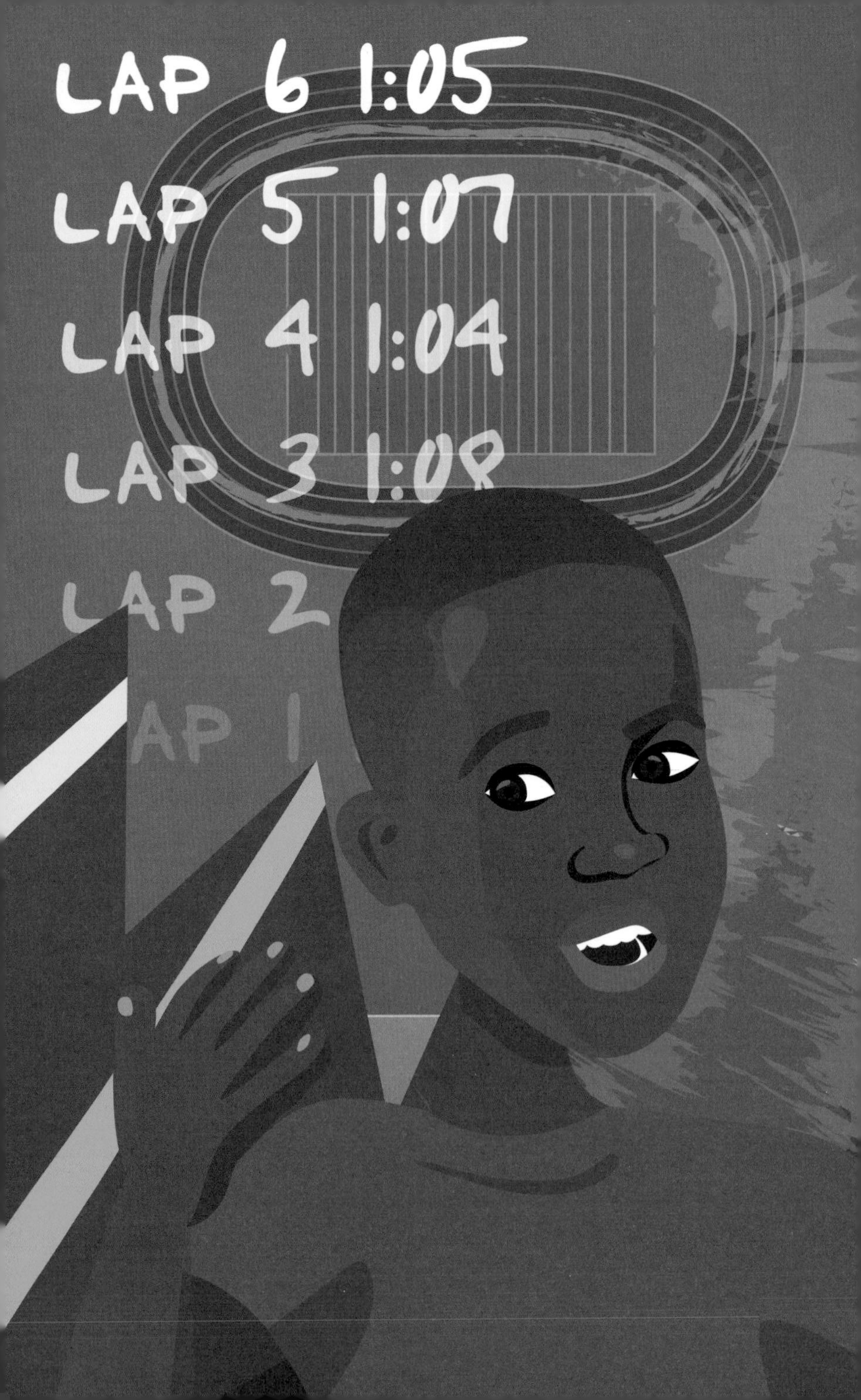
LAP 6 1:05
LAP 5 1:07
LAP 4 1:04
LAP 3 1:08
LAP 2
AP 1

Chapter 29

Vontae Sleeps In

Football season is in the fall. But Coach Craig strongly suggests his football players do something athletic in the spring.

"I want you to run track," Coach Craig tells his team.

Nearly all the boys groan. The idea of running outside after school on hot, D.C. spring afternoons does not sound fun. But Coach Craig likes the head track coach. His name is Isaac Parker, and he was an accomplished middle-distance sprinter. Parker twice competed at the U.S. Olympic Trials in the 800-meter race. Coach Parker has a command of proper running mechanics. That means helping each person run his or her top speed because of great form. That is useful to *all* Crimson Tide athletes, Coach Craig believes.

In fact, Coach Parker has already done wonders with a linebacker named Luke Cain. The Crimson Tide linebacker could run the 40-yard dash in 4.9 seconds. But after working for an entire spring with Coach Parker, Cain shaves four-tenths of a second off his time. That is significantly faster, enough to compel major colleges to start pursuing Cain.

Track practices are long and painful. And track meets are even worse! The athletes are there all day just to run for a few minutes in their respective races.

With his natural speed, Vontae does well in track. But he does not enjoy the sport. So, one Saturday, Vontae decides to sleep in and skip the meet. He is sore from Friday's practice, and he is extra tired after playing video games past his 10:30 p.m. bedtime.

At 9 a.m., Grandma enters Vontae's room.

"Tae, don't you have a track meet this morning?" she asks him.

Vontae rolls away from the door.

"No, Momma," he says. "Not today."

Twenty minutes later, the house phone rings. Grandma answers.

"Hello," she says in a pleasant voice. "Oh, hello Coach Parker. How are you?"

Vontae sits up in his bed. He knows he is about to be in big trouble!

"What do you mean, 'Where is Vontae?'" Grandma says. "He says there's no meet today."

Grandma does not speak for a moment, soaking in whatever Coach Parker is telling her. Vontae knows it's the truth—and that's not good for him.

"Well thank you for calling, Coach Parker," Grandma says nicely.

Barely a second passes before her tone changes.

"Vontae!" Grandma screams. "Get down here right *now!*"

Vontae hustles out of bed and scrambles down the stairs and into the living room.

"Yes?" he asks sheepishly.

"You need to tell me something?" she asks.

Vontae knows his only hope is to immediately own up to his lie.

"Momma, I'm sorry," he says. "I don't like track, and I was real tired this morning."

Grandma shakes her head and furrows her lips.

"We will talk about the punishment later," she says, "but I want you to get to the track meet right away. You cannot let Coach Parker and your teammates down."

Vontae quickly gathers his track bag and rushes out the door. When he gets to the meet, Coach Parker motions for him to approach.

"Vontae, I know you don't like to run," Coach Parker says, "but I'm disappointed with you. You have talent, and your team was counting on you. I know you were not planning to compete today, but you're going to run the 800 for us."

Vontae cannot imagine a worse punishment! He normally practices with the sprinters, in the 100- and 200-meter races. But as a sophomore, he does not always get to compete at meets in the individual 100- and 200-meter races. There are sometimes limits on how many athletes can compete from each school, and there are two older teammates who are better than Vontae. For now, he just runs in the 100- and 200-meter relay races, which features four sprinters.

The 100- and 200-meters are not even a full lap around a typical high school track. But the 800 is two whole laps!

The race is punishing on the body, like a sprint for nearly half a mile. Coach Parker can see that Vontae is not thrilled to run the 800.

Coach Parker's Rule

"Whether you want to do something or not, push yourself to finish and do your best," Coach says.

Vontae slowly nods his head. Fortunately, he has some time to prepare for the 800. There are several other events before that one. Watching others compete, Vontae decides he will push himself and see what happens.

When the race starts, he takes a quick lead. But after 250 meters, Vontae's legs start to burn, and competitors start to catch up to him. Halfway through the race, two others pass him. Then, in the final straightaway, Vontae pumps his arms and legs as fast as they'll go. He focuses on the finish line and stops paying attention to his competition.

When he crosses the line, Vontae looks up at the results board.

Five others finish ahead of him. He only defeats two competitors.

Vontae collapses to the ground, completely exhausted. He starts the day tired, and he finishes the day even more tired. But instead of shame, Vontae feels pride. Coach Parker made him do something he did not want to do, and Vontae performs admirably, especially since this is his first time competing in the 800.

Chapter 30

Coach Craig Inspires

Vontae works his way into the lineup as a sophomore. Coaches catch glimpses of his immense potential. In one game, Vontae saves a touchdown by chasing down a highly-recruited receiver from another team.

"Wow, I can't believe he caught him," Coach Craig says to Coach Cox. "That kid is going to be playing Division I football next season!"

But there are cringe-worthy moments too. Vontae makes mistakes during plays that really hurt the Crimson Tide.

Coach Cox is gruff and tough, and very emotional. But Coach Craig, the head coach, is always laid back. He always seems to be calm, no matter how tight a game may be.

Coach Craig graduated from Dunbar, and he played football at Cheyney University, a historically black college about an hour west of Philadelphia. After college, Coach Craig plays semi-pro football and earns a tryout with the Atlanta Falcons. But his pro football career does not last very long, and he returns to the D.C. area to start teaching and coaching.

Coach Craig wants to build a championship team, but he cares more about developing young champions. He shares inspiring

quotes and gives them positive messages. Coach Craig brings in lots of guest speakers, men respected in the community and committed to helping others.

One regular visitor is Steve Fitzhugh. After playing in college, he plays a few games for the Denver Broncos. Fitzhugh works with the Fellowship of Christian Athletes, a national sports ministry. He talks about the Bible, sports, and life.

Fitzhugh is a fiery speaker, and he has lots of memorable sayings.

"Any dead fish can go with the flow," Fitzhugh tells the students. "It takes a strong fish to go up the stream."

His challenge to the Dunbar athletes is to do what is right, not just to follow what others are doing.

"Embrace your uniqueness," he says.

That's where Coach Craig really helps Vontae. For all his natural gifts in the classroom and on the field, Vontae struggles with good choices and habits.

Coach Craig sets high expectations for everyone. Players must be on time, which means actually arriving to meetings and practices 10 minutes early. Schoolwork is checked daily, so no one falls behind in any classes. Players must wear Dunbar's official red-and-black workout attire, or else they will sit out the entire

practice and miss part of the next game. Everyone stretches in a particular sequence, and they must do so as one unit. And Coach Craig schedules everything down to the minute, from how long they spend on each technique to when they take water breaks.

Some players jokingly refer to Coach Craig as a drill sergeant. Those military leaders are known for being very precise and demanding!

Whenever he speaks, Coach Craig talks about accountability, character, work ethic, and time management.

As his sophomore football season ends, Vontae is summoned to Coach Craig's office for a chat.

"Vontae, you are doing fine," Coach Craig says. "But you are not an average student or athlete. I see greatness in you. To get there, you need to really learn to focus."

Coach Craig's Rule

"If you can't be trusted to do the little things off the field, you can't be trusted to do the big things on the field."

Vontae wants more playing time and to become a starter. And he also wants to follow in his brother's footsteps and go to college. Vontae wants to be the player Coach Craig envisions he can be.

Chapter 31

The Gift of Shoes

Vontae does not have a lot of free time in high school. His days are packed with classes and practices. His evenings are filled with homework and extra workouts. Dunbar is demanding, which is why so many graduates go on to college.

The expectations are different at Roosevelt High School, where many of Vontae's neighborhood friends go. The graduation rate at Roosevelt is considerably lower than Dunbar, and there are not as many resources and specialists. Each week, it seems Vontae hears about someone who drops out of Roosevelt or gets in trouble with the police. These updates always make him sad.

Vontae still tries to make time to see his friend Carl. In fact, Carl tries to attend most of Vontae's basketball and football games, and even some of his track meets. After all, they still share a passion for basketball and video games.

After his sophomore year, Vontae applies for different jobs in the area. He is determined to earn some money so he can have his own spending money to buy snacks, new clothes, and to purchase the latest edition of NBA Live, the popular basketball game. The game will cost him over $50! He will have to work long and hard to save up that much money.

Vontae applies for four jobs. A week later, he finds out that he has two offers. One is washing dishes in a local sandwich shop. The other is monitoring small kids as part of a summer-long program.

He prefers to be outside, so Vontae decides to work with kids. The job requires him to work four hours a day, four days a week. Vontae and two other student helpers work with two adult leaders to manage over 60 kids ages 5–11.

The goal is to control the chaos. Often the students and adults are overmatched by the unruly kids. Vontae does his best to settle them down and keep them calm. But they scream, run, push, and wreak havoc wherever they go. When his work time ends, Vontae walks home and collapses on the couch. The kids wear him out!

On Wednesdays, Vontae does not have to work, and he usually hangs out with Carl. The two, of course, favor video games and play basketball at different outdoor courts near them. They are a skilled duo and other kids want to play with them. Other teams rarely defeat them because of Vontae's speed to the basket and Carl's outside shooting. Midway through the summer, Carl stops wanting to play basketball.

"Nah, you can go without me," Carl tells Vontae at his front door one Wednesday. "I don't feel like playing."

Other days, Carl tells Vontae that a different body part hurts.

"Carl, what's wrong?" Vontae asks. "You love basketball! And you're not even leaving the house."

For several days, Vontae plays basketball without Carl. But it's just not the same. It's not as much fun.

On his next day off, Vontae again swings by Carl's house. They play video games for a while, and then Vontae gets up to head out to play hoops.

"Let's go, Carl," Vontae says.

"Nah, I'm good," Carl says.

"Carl, something's not right," Vontae says. "What's really going on?"

Carl lowers his head. He decides to tell his friend the truth. He turns his palms up toward the ceiling and speaks softly.

"Truth is, my basketball shoes don't fit anymore," Carl says. "I've outgrown them, and my mom can't afford to buy me a new pair. The only shoes that fit are my church shoes."

Vontae feels bad for his friend. He decides to skip basketball that day and continues to play video games with Carl.

The following week, on his day off, Vontae returns to Carl's house. When Carl answers the door, Vontae immediately motions for his friend to follow him.

"Let's go," Vontae tells Carl. "I've got a surprise for you."

THE GIFT OF SHOES

Carl does not want to leave the house, especially in his church shoes. Since he is not playing basketball, Carl uncomfortably squeezes into his old basketball shoes.

"Where are we going, Vontae?" Carl asks.

Vontae does not answer. He walks a few blocks, two steps ahead of Carl. They do not speak. Vontae approaches a Foot Locker. He opens the door to the store and holds it open for Carl. Once inside, Vontae pulls a bunch of cash out of his pocket.

"I've been saving up money to buy NBA Live," Vontae says. "But I'd rather use the money to buy you some new shoes so we can play basketball together again."

Carl looks stunned.

Vontae starts to look over the shoe selection and points to different ones.

"What do you think of these?" Vontae asks Carl.

Vontae does not have enough money to buy Carl the latest pair of Michael Jordan's, which cost over $100. But there are still a lot of good options within his budget. Carl makes his selection after looking at 40 different pair and trying some on. He picks a pair of Jordan's from a previous year that are on sale.

Carl asks the sales associate to throw out his old pair of shoes and wears his new ones right out of the store. Carl, of course, keeps the shiny black Jordan box.

"Thanks, Vontae," Carl says. "I can't believe you did this. Now let's go find us a game to dominate. I gotta break these shoes in."

For Vontae, the enjoyment of the video game can wait. Surprising and helping his friend feels way better.

Coach Criticizes Vontae

Vontae likes Coach Craig. When Coach Craig speaks, he encourages others and recites philosophical sayings from famous people Vontae has never heard of. Coach Craig also recognizes that Vontae is sensitive, so he does not criticize him in front of others. If he has an issue with Vontae, Coach Craig summons him into his office for a private talk.

Vontae does not like Coach Cox, however. When he speaks, Coach Cox blames and shames, often peppering his comments with bad words Vontae is not allowed to utter. If Vontae makes a mistake in a game, Coach Cox takes him off the field to yell at him. If Vontae makes a mistake in a practice, Coach Cox calls him out and orders him to backpedal 100 yards while berating him.

Coach Cox commands through fear. The players aim to please him because, once in a while, he will mumble a compliment or offer a simple fist bump with a small smile. But those instances are rare—and they're never directed at Vontae.

Vontae cannot escape Coach Cox. He is the defensive backs' coach, and Vontae plays safety and cornerback.

Heading into his junior year, Vontae becomes one of the team's key players. But no one would know it listening to Coach

RUN!
FASTER!
Go!

Cox. During a conditioning session, Vontae's toe misses the sideline by a yard. From halfway across the field, Coach Cox blasts Vontae for trying to cheat.

"You don't have to be out here, Vontae!" Coach Cox yells. "You can go home and watch your big brother on TV."

The words pierce him deeply.

It's true, Vernon is nine miles away, in College Park, Maryland, where he is a star for the University of Maryland. He does not shine in as many positions as he did at Dunbar, but Vernon is still one of the most versatile and dominant athletes in all of college football. His rare combination of size and speed enables him to line up in the backfield as a fullback, and to play tight end and wide receiver. He also returns kickoffs!

Of course, Vontae cheers on his brother. But Coach Cox's comments are meant to hurt his feelings... and they do.

That night at dinner, Vontae tells his family that he is thinking of quitting the football team.

"The coach cussed at me," Vontae says, "and he picks on me more than everyone else. I don't have to put up with that!"

Grandma gently shakes her head.

"I would think twice about that, Tae," she says.

Between bites, Vontae peeks up and looks at Grandma. He knows some wisdom is about to flow out of her mouth.

"He should not be saying bad words to you and that is something you should respectfully talk to him about," Grandma says. "If he doesn't listen to you, then I'll have a talk with him. But if you love to play football, you should keep on playing. The question you need to ask yourself is: are you going to let him rule your life?"

Vontae resumes chewing his food as he reflects on what Grandma says.

"Well, he is pretty mean to everyone," Vontae says. "But I do learn a lot from him."

Grandma nods her head.

"Maybe he sees something in you," she says, "and he is trying to bring that out."

She pauses then adds her final thought.

Grandma's Rule

"God don't make mistakes. Have faith and look for the lesson," she says.

Once again, Vontae feels encouragement from Grandma. He likes the way Coach Craig talks to him and encourages him, and he trusts all the people Coach Craig brings around the team, from speakers to assistants.

"There's no one Coach Craig trusts more than Coach Cox," Vontae says. "Maybe I do need to listen to him more."

Even if he doesn't always like Coach Cox, Vontae still wants to play for Coach Craig.

Chapter 33

Vernon Teaches Vontae a Lesson

Vontae works his way into Dunbar's starting lineup, and his relationship with Coach Cox improves. But Coach Craig still does not believe Vontae is maximizing his potential on the football field. Vontae possesses natural athleticism and talent, but he is inconsistent. He dominates in one game against a tough opponent. Then he gives up big plays in the next game to a lesser opponent.

Coach Craig and Coach Cox try to get the message through to Vontae. But Vontae does not fully embrace their input. Coach Craig knows who can get through to Vontae.

One Saturday morning, Vontae is fast asleep when someone bursts into his bedroom at 5 a.m.

"Get up!" Vernon says, shaking his little brother hard. "Get these workout clothes on right now."

Vontae is exhausted; he likes to sleep in on Saturday mornings, usually past at least 8:30 a.m. But Vernon plucks Vontae out of bed, and he starts to take off his pajama shirt for him.

Vontae takes over and finishes dressing himself. Then he follows Vernon down to the living room. The television is already on with a video on pause.

"Coach Craig tells me you are having some effort and technique problems," Vernon says. "I had the weekend off, so I'm gonna make sure we fix that."

Vontae gets defensive.

"They don't know what they're talking about!" Vontae says. "I'm not having those problems."

Vernon grabs the remote control.

"I figured you'd say that," Vernon says.

"Look at this play," Vernon says, unpausing the video. "Look, that receiver is smaller than you, and he is knocking you off the line of scrimmage! Are you serious?"

Vontae rubs his eyes. The video does show him getting physically handled on the play. Vernon fast-forwards to a different play against a different opponent.

"Let's see this one," Vernon says. "Look at how upright you are. You can get away with that against some weak high school players, but any college football player at any level is gonna embarrass you when you're not in your athletic position!"

Vernon shows Vontae his athletic stance. Vontae is wide awake now. The video clips get his heart rate up. He does not like to see his own lowlights. Vernon fast-forwards to another play. Vontae knows that Coach Craig has not only talked to Vernon, he has also handed him this specially-edited video!

Vernon shows a play in which a receiver stiff-arms Vontae on the side of his helmet. (This is when a player straightens his arm and uses it to legally shield off the defender.) After pushing him away for a moment, the receiver separates from Vontae and cruises another 15 yards into the end zone.

"No, no, no!" Vernon says loudly. "Where is your effort? You can't play defense like that! He hits you with that stiff arm, then you gotta bounce back and take him down, not let him score."

Vernon shakes his head.

"So you still think your coaches don't know what they're talking about?" Vernon asks Vontae.

Vontae doesn't say a word.

"Vontae, college has been great," Vernon says. "I am learning a lot, I'm making friends, and I get to play ball. Everyone is telling me that I'm going to the NFL and that I could be a first-round pick. Can you believe that?"

Vontae nods his head.

"Of course you are, Vernon," Vontae says. "You're the best athlete I know!"

Vernon gives him a respectful head nod back.

"Wanna know something?" Vernon asks his brother.

"What's that?" Vontae responds.

"I know that you're good enough to get a football scholarship and also play in the NFL," he says. "I know what you're capable of. Follow me. I gotta show you something."

Vernon heads for the front door. Vontae follows. When they get to the front, Vernon starts to jog at a brisk pace.

After five minutes, they arrive at Roosevelt High School. Vernon is still fresh; Vontae needs a break.

"No time to rest," Vernon says, heading for the silver bleachers. "That was just a warmup run."

Vernon sprints up the 12 flights of bleachers, then he runs back down.

"Your turn," Vernon says, between heavy breaths.

Vontae starts fast, but he slows halfway up. Then, even on the descent, he is barely at a jogging pace.

"Again," Vernon says, jetting up the bleachers.

They repeat the bleacher run four more times. Vontae collapses onto the grass, when Vernon mercifully tells him they are done.

"I want you to jog here and run these stairs three times a week," Vernon tells him.

Vontae shakes his head, as he chugs the last two gulps of water from their bottle.

Vernon's Rule

"You can always get better. When you're sitting at home, someone else is working," Vernon says.

Vontae thinks about all the players he faces and all the players he knows. They all *want* to play college football. But he realizes that he is in one of thousands of communities through the United States.

"Vontae, you need to get tougher, stronger, and learn to work harder," Vernon says. "Because talent isn't enough."

Vontae remembers Vernon going for early-morning runs and doing late-night workouts in the basement. He'd do hundreds of push-ups, sit-ups, and squats.

"I always felt my competitors were outworking me," Vernon says. "Don't let other people outwork you for this opportunity."

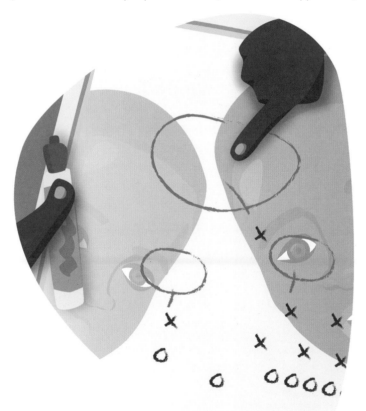

Chapter 34

Carving His Own Path

Vontae finishes his junior season strong, rising to his brother's challenge to put in extra work. The payoff is evident in spring track, when he starts to earn some bronze medals in the 100- and 200-meter sprints and helps the 4x100 relay team win meets. A few small colleges show interest in Vontae.

But his focus is on making the most of his senior year, and Vontae knows that hard work starts in the summer. So, by himself, he does early morning workouts at Roosevelt High School four days a week.

He turns heads at a seven-on-seven football tournament in Virginia. Vontae dominates, both as a defensive back and a receiver. Then, at the State College Nike Camp, he really introduces himself to top collegiate programs.

Vontae shows off a 33-inch vertical leap, which is nearly three feet off the ground. But perhaps more important, he runs the 40-yard dash in 4.4 seconds! That time puts him in elite company.

During summer track, Vontae works on more explosive starts in the sprints. That improvement helps him transform bronze medals in the 100- and 200-meter dashes into gold medals!

Heading into his final football season, Vontae makes a bold decision: he passes up No. 18, the number Vernon wore. Instead, he picks No. 4.

"Coach Craig, I want to be my own person," Vontae tells Coach. "You're going to see a different Vontae Davis this year."

Coach Craig nods and smiles.

"I've always known you have it in you, Vontae," Coach Craig says. "I can't wait!"

Coach Craig is so impressed with Vontae he decides the senior will play defense *and* offense. Where his conditioning had been a problem in the past season, Vontae never tires anymore, even though he plays a lot more snaps. More impressive is the fact that Vontae now consistently plays at a high level.

The Crimson Tide open the football season well, and Grandma and Grandpa start to hear the home phone ring a lot—college coaches want to learn more about Vontae. Vontae refuses to get distracted. He wants to help Dunbar have a memorable season, which must include a Turkey Bowl win.

Dunbar heads into that illustrious game with an 8-1 record. They must defeat a dangerous team from Coolidge High School.

The game is hard fought on a rainy night. With three minutes remaining, and the Crimson Tide protecting a 24-20 lead, Vontae is on the receiving end of a stiff arm from a Coolidge receiver. Coolidge earns a key first down. Vontae does not back down.

On the next play, the quarterback fakes a run, then tries to throw a slant pass to his receiver. Vontae gets a great jump on the ball, and he steps in front of the receiver. He intercepts the pass! Vontae runs toward the right sideline, dodging two offensive players. But the running back throws himself at Vontae's legs and trips him up.

Vontae's clutch play secures another Turkey Bowl victory for Dunbar!

Vontae's season is a brilliant one: He leads all D.C. players with

eight interceptions, and he also catches 25 passes for 612 yards.

With his season complete, Vontae shifts his attention to where he will play his next football season. Several big colleges—Virginia, Illinois, Michigan State, and Maryland—offer him a full athletic scholarship.

Should he follow in his brother's footsteps and head to Maryland? Vontae likes the idea, since the Terrapin home games are within an hour for family members. Besides, Vernon leaves Maryland after his junior season and winds up the sixth overall pick in the 2006 NFL Draft. But should Vontae chart his own path at one of the other colleges? They are all further away from home and family but offer a new adventure.

Vontae is the No. 1 recruit in the D.C. area, so Coach Craig organizes a press conference for Vontae to announce his college choice. Friends, relatives, classmates, and local reporters show up to Dunbar's gym to hear Vontae sign his National Letter of Intent. (That's a document a high school athlete must sign to make a college's scholarship offer official.)

Vontae is nervous to have so many people waiting to hear what he says. But he gains confidence because those he loves the most are there to cheer on his decision. It's such a big day, Grandma wears a dress she usually only wears on Easter!

Vontae sits at a table that features a baseball hat from each of the four colleges. He clears his throat.

"I want to thank my family for helping me reach this special moment," Vontae says. "And I also want to thank my coaches and teammates for making my time with the Crimson Tide so special."

There is applause.

"This was a tough decision," Vontae continues. "These are all great schools for academics and sports. But I've decided to play college football for Coach Zook at the University of Illinois!"

Vontae grabs the baseball hat with an orange "I" on it and puts it on his head. He flashes his big smile. Vontae remembers Coach Zook from when he visited Vernon a few years earlier. At the time, Coach Zook was at the University of Florida. Vontae thinks Coach Zook is a nice man and a good coach.

This is one of the proudest days of his life.

Epilogue

Vontae maintains his momentum from his senior year at Dunbar High School. Immediately transitioning from high school to college is difficult. Vontae plays for the Fighting Illini as a true freshman, and he records 30 tackles and intercepts one pass. He is named to the Freshman All-America first team by multiple media outlets.

In 2007, he starts all 12 games, records 56 tackles, and intercepts four passes. He helps the Illini get the chance to play in the famed Rose Bowl. Though his team loses the game, Vontae finishes the game with team-best and career-high 13 tackles. For his brilliant season, Vontae is an All-Big Ten first-team honoree and is named a semifinalist for the Jim Thorpe Award, given to the nation's top defensive back. He is the only sophomore on the list.

As a junior, he is a first-team All-Big Ten honoree and Jim Thorpe Award semifinalist again, as well a third-team Rivals.com All-American. He is also named the Big Ten's Best Athlete by the Sporting News. He foregoes his senior year and declares for the 2009 NFL Draft.

Between the NFL Combine and the Illini's Pro Day, Vontae once again showcases his athleticism. With the 25th overall pick in the first round, the Miami Dolphins select Vontae. He immediately earns his way onto the field, and he makes his first career interception on Oct. 4th, in a 38-10 victory over the Buffalo Bills. Not only does he pick off the pass, Vontae also returns it 23 yards for a touchdown!

Less than a month later, Vontae starts his first NFL game. In Week 9, Vontae intercepts future Hall of Fame quarterback Tom Brady.

Pro Football Weekly selects Vontae to its All-Rookie team.

Vontae becomes a regular starter, but the Dolphins trade him to the Indianapolis Colts in August 2012. He immediately starts for the Colts, and he helps the Colts qualify for the postseason. On January 6, 2013, Vontae makes his first career playoff start, though the Colts lose 24-9 to the Baltimore Ravens, the eventual Super Bowl champion.

He dominates in 2013, starting all 16 games and notching 46 tackles, 12 pass deflections and an interception. But there's one extra special game: Week 3 against the San Francisco 49ers. Vernon is a star for the 49ers, and it provides the brothers their first chance to line up against each other on the football field. Vernon does not play because of a hamstring injury—the only game he misses that season—and the Colts prevail 27-7. The Colts win the AFC South, and Vontae helps them win a playoff game.

In 2014, Vontae earns his first selection to the Pro Bowl: the NFL's All-Star game. According to Pro Football Focus, Vontae grades as the second-best cornerback with an overall rating of 95.1, and he does not give up a single touchdown. Vontae makes the Pro Bowl again after the 2015 season and ranks as the third-best cornerback.

Vontae faces his brother again in 2015, after Vernon is traded from the 49ers to the Denver Broncos during the season. But it is Vernon's first game for the Broncos, and he is targeted on just one pass. Vontae, meanwhile, has three tackles in a 27-24 Colts victory.

Vontae misses two starts in 2016, and he struggles with a groin injury in 2017 that requires surgery. After six seasons, Vontae's time with the Colts comes to an end. In February 2018, Vontae signs a one-year contract with the Buffalo Bills. But he battles to stay healthy and only makes one start.

"It's more important for me to walk away healthy," Vontae says in a statement, "than willfully embrace the warrior mentality and limp away too late."

Vontae does not just see himself as a football player.

He is thankful for all the opportunities football has provided him. But he is excited about his future with his wife Megan, whom he married in 2015. And he is excited about investing in and building businesses.

"It's so crazy," Vontae says. "Everything was overwhelming when I first retired. Now I have time to see what really motivates me. One of the things I want to do is help other people. I am living my purpose to make an impact on this world."

Vontae regularly volunteered throughout his life, including in the NFL. With the Colts, he supported Hands of Hope, an organization focused on aiding orphans through adoption and foster care.

"I want to be a mentor and role model to kids who didn't grow up with father figures," Vontae says. "There are too many kids who have that story."

Vontae's Life Rule

"Do not compare yourself to others. My grandmother never compares me and my siblings. We all have different relationships with her for that reason and that's a beautiful thing. She accepts each of us for who we are, and we all accept each other. Make sure to focus on what you have and make the best of your opportunities."